St.Briavel's Castle

The Most Haunted Building in the World

Part One

St.Briavel's Castle

The Castle looking less scary in the glorious sunlight

Contents

Introduction, and a Brief History of the Castle

About the Author, and Ghost Hunting

The Castle Maps
The First and Second Floors, The Castle Grounds, The Top Floors

Chapter 1 - The East Tower
- The Stairs and Corridors
Noisy Children, Running Water and Automatic Lights
- The Oubliette
The Scary Bed, Fluctuating Temperature, BOL's, The Ghost That Likes To Stroke, If You're Happy and You Know It Clap Your Hands, Disembodied Voices, Rattling Chains and Padlocks, Mary and Elizabeth, The Footsteps, The Dark Shadow, Under the Doorway

Chapter 2 - The East Tower
- The Constable's Room
The BOL, Attack of the Ghostly Lurgy, Noisy Doors, The Shaky Bed, Ghost Rustlers,

Chapter 3 - The East Tower
- The Chaplain's Room
More Footsteps, The Dark Figures, The Flasher, The Ghost That Likes To Stroke Part Two, The Affluent Spirit, The Bed Mover, The Twitching Curtains, The Talking Man, Get Out of Bed, Warm Breath

The start of a Ghost Hunt featuring the world famous ghost hunter Mr C.J Romer, seen here walking out to the car park.

Chapter 4 - The West Tower
- The Hanging Room and the Guard Room
The Screaming Man, The Figure in the Doorway, Marbles, EMF results, The Pusher, The Ghost That Likes To Stroke Part Three, The Opening Windows, Scrying, More Footsteps, The Neck Toucher Strikes Again, The Pusher Part Two, The Shadow With a Voice, Bols and Mist, The Tapping Window, Witnesses From Foreign Fields, What a Mess, The Moving Beds, Heavy Breathing, Hahaha, The Moving Box, The Shadow Moves, The Footsteps Upstairs, Flashers in the Hanging Room, Pinch Me Please, Phantom Footsteps, The Guard Room Blue Flasher,

Chapter 5 - The West Tower
- The Prison
Footsteps Again, The Moving Wardrobe, Voices From The Other Side (of the fire exit), The Dark Shadow, Grabbed By A Ghoulie, Ghostly Growls, Phantom Breezes, BOL's, Whistlers,

Chapter 6 - The West Tower
- The Porter's Lodge
The Ever Opening Door, I Can't Get Out Of Bed, The Figure Near The Fireplace, The Rolling Coin, The Figure in the Doorway, Dragging, The Crying Baby,

- The Old Kitchen
Your Friendly Neighbourhood Poltergeist - Called Tom, A Handy Apparition, More People Than There Should Be, I Said Get Out Of My Chair, Pinch Me, The Sofa Sitter, Let's Open A Bank

Chapter 7 - The West Tower
- The Upstairs Corridors and Stairs
The Ratting Door, The Noisy Stairs, The Falling Stones,

Chapter 8 - The Great Hall
- The State Apartments / Corridor Isobel's room
Many Many Footsteps, The Woman and Girl In White, The Violins, Angry Arguments, Lights and Mist, The Woman on the Battlements, Phantom Pillow Flinging, Don't Touch Me

Chapter 9 - The Main Castle
- King John's Lounge
The Crying Child, The Floaters, Red Roger,

Chapter 10 - The Main Castle
- The Chapel
The Chapel Doors, The Noisy Ghosts,

Chapter 11 - The Main Castle
- Reception, The stairs, Corridors, and Toilets
Name Calling, Desperate for the Loo, The Castle Pets, The Most Haunted Staircase,

Chapter 12 - The Main Castle
- The Refectory, The Gatehouse
Is it A Peeping Tom?, The Rattling doors, Phantom Horses, The Floating Legs, The Banging on the Floor, The Banging Doors, Knock, Knock, Who's There?

Chapter 13 - The Castle Grounds
- The Gardens, The Car Park, The George in the Moat
The Knight In Shining Armour, The Skulking Figure, The Ghost That is George, The Graveyard, Other Village Ghosts,

Chapter 14 - What To Do If You See A Ghost

Chapter 15 - Conclusion, Epilogue, and Rest In Peace

Chapter 16 - More History

Introduction, and a Very Brief History of the Castle

St.Briavel's castle a magnificent castle that is hundreds, (very nearly a thousand) years old. So is this the most haunted building in the World? In my opinion most definitely. So why is this book entitled St.Briavel's Castle - The Most Haunted Building in the World - PART ONE? Well at the time of writing this book I was going through the thousands of stories we have been given, and trying to cut it down to a workable figure to include in this volume. I realised to include every story this book would be about 1000 pages long. I can also state with a great deal of certainty that by the time you have read this book there will have been several more sightings and reports. This is the reason the book is called 'PART ONE'. I know full well there are enough stories already for a 'Part Two,'; and by the time this is printed I could well be onto enough for a part three.

This book will take you on a walk around the castle and tell you all about the ghosts and paranormal activity that have happened in each room. There have been hundreds of reports of ghosts in this castle over the years. We will limit ourselves to stories that happen on regular occasions or ones that have happened in the last 10 years (this book was written and published in 2010). If we included every story, of every ghost then this book would be bigger than the Encyclopaedia Britannica.

I will add a longer section on the history at the back of the book but I know we are all itching to get on with some spook spotting so ghosties first.

Not looking so friendly now in the cold dark days of winter

WARNING!

If you have bought a copy of this book whilst you are at the castle can I suggest you get a good nights sleep before you read this, and maybe give yourself a ghost tour in the morning after breakfast, I cannot be held responsible for you being so scared that you don't sleep. The castle is currently a youth hostel so if you have bought this book and would like to stay in a haunted building this is probably your best chance to experience anything paranormal. If you have booked to stay at the castle and you have got so scared after the first night please make sure you tell the staff all about the ghosts you hear or see, as they keep a ghost book of everything that goes on.

The castle ruins are just as haunted as all the bedrooms

This castle has not always been a youth hostel, and we think that there have been fortified buildings on this site for over one thousand years, so if you believe in ghosts it is highly likely that there should be one here. It has had many uses over its rather grizzly history, some more scary than others, it has been a prison, a place of execution, a factory for making weapons, and there are the less scary times, when it has been a youth hostel, a private home, or the scariest of all a private school!

A brief hello from our neighbours in the graveyard

About the Author and Ghost Hunting

Ross Andrews has written several books, magazine articles, appeared on TV and radio, and been interviewed countless times about hauntings and ghosts throughout the UK. In his opinion St.Briavel's castle has to be the most haunted building in the whole of the world. No other building boasts as many haunting's that happen as regularly as they do in this amazing historic residence.

If you are staying in the castle and wish to visit other haunted places then I recommend Ross Andrews' Paranormal Forest of Dean, as it will show you a multitude of places to visit all within about 10 miles of the castle. You are less than five miles from Clearwell Caves which is also haunted, Puzzlewood which has had reports of Roman ghosts, and several pubs surrounding this beautiful area, in fact why not visit the George Inn, situated in the moat of the castle, they serve delicious food, and it is also haunted.

Ross has been a ghost hunter for almost twenty years at the time of writing this book, and has investigated all over the UK and the occasional paranormal trip into other parts of Europe. Various appearances on TV and radio, make him the ideal person to guide you around this great castle.

So what is a ghost? And how will you know if you have found one?

Many people have different ideas of what a ghost is, some people will say that it is a spirit that has comeback from the dead due to some unfinished business that it has to carry out. Maybe it was someone who was murdered and is trying to tell people who the killer was, or perhaps it was someone who buried all their jewellery to keep it safe and is trying to get people to pass it on to their loved ones, maybe it is someone trying to warn others away from somewhere dangerous so that they do not die in the same way. All of those reasons are related to real life haunting, and often once the ghost's purpose has been fulfilled it then disappears.

Other people think that a ghost is no more than a video recording somehow caught in the atmosphere that replays over and over again, when the weather conditions are right or the atmospheric pressure is the same then a 'time slip' can happen and the viewer sees what happened on that very spot in history.

There are as many theories, as there are ghosts in this world, as to what they are. More importantly is that they do exist, lots of sceptics will say that you are mad to believe in them, and these people tend to have a very narrow view of what a ghost may be. It is impossible to say ghosts do not exist as so many people have seen them, what we have to address is WHAT IS A GHOST?

Floor plans of the Castle

GROUND FLOOR

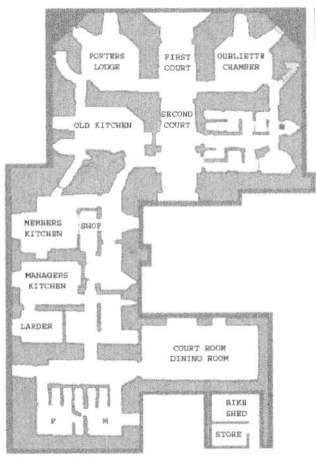

Map of the Ground Floor of the Castle

FIRST FLOOR

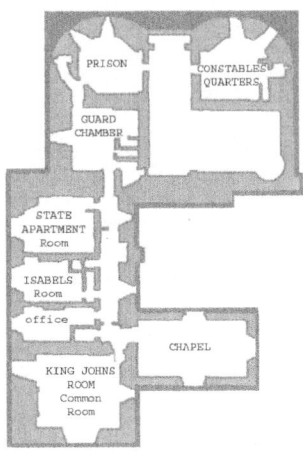

Map of the first floor of the castle

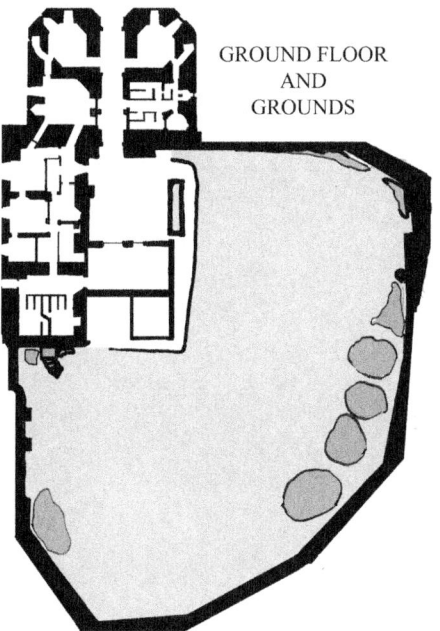

GROUND FLOOR AND GROUNDS

The Upper Floors East Tower Chaplain's Room
The West Tower Hanging Room and Guard Room

The Top Floors of Both Towers
Chaplains Room, Guard Room, and Hanging Room

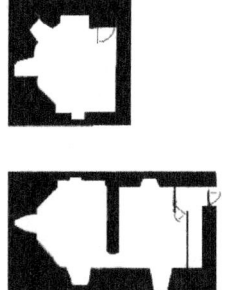

Accommodation provided to those who do not pay their bills

Chapter 1 - The East Tower

The view of the East Tower as seen from the pond in the now filled in Moat

So if you are stood outside the castle looking in, then the East tower is the one on the left hand side, if you walk through the large double doors you will see a red door on your left and one on your right, the one on the left is actually the fire exit from the Oubliette room, which I shall come onto very shortly. The one on your right is the fire exit to the Porters Lodge room, this is unsurprisingly the West Tower, but we shall talk about that later on in the book. Let us, for now, concern ourselves primarily with the East Tower.

Ignore these two doors and a few more feet along the wall on the left you will see a low door, and a corridor often blocked by a wooden portcullis style gate. If the gate is open then venture through it and around the corner pass the toilets, showers and drying room, and at the bottom of the stairs you will see the Oubliette room.

Before we walk into the Oubliette room, let me point out that you must not fall into the trap of thinking that the bedrooms are the only haunted areas in this amazing building. Why should a ghost only haunt a bedroom, they have no reason to stick to one place and are often found roaming all over the castle. The East Tower has a prime example of the wandering ghosties. Why not sit down on the bottom of the stairs as you read this next section.

The view of the East Tower from the moat

The Stairs and Corridors of the East Tower

Noisy Children

Many school groups, and youth organisations come and stay at the castle which is superb, as primarily this is its intended use, it is only since the early years of the 'noughties' that Ghost hunting has become an en vogue hobby, mostly due to the success of television shows like 'Most Haunted', and television mediums such as Derek Accorah. Regardless of what our personal opinions are of these television entertainments, they have done a great deal for ghost hunting publicity and this building has benefited greatly.

Are you sitting comfortably? Then I shall begin

The reason I tell you this is that I think it is best to get that out in the open before anyone accuses us of trying to drum up publicity through fanciful tales of haunting. The stories I am going to talk about in this book, happen again and again, and are reported not just by ghost hunters, but by all the regular visitors to this glorious building. School groups, and youth groups, are notorious for telling ghost stories to try and scare each other, but they also tell us about the haunting that they often encounter. We could take these stories with a pinch of salt and say of course it is just children making up tales and trying to scare one another, but when these stories come from children in different schools, and yet they seem to agree with each other, it is harder to dismiss. The best stories however come not from the children, but from the teachers and youth workers themselves, they often try to play down the haunting aspect as obviously a castle full of frightened, tired, and mischievous children are not very conducive to a decent nights sleep.

The most commonly occurring story involves children; many teachers refuse to even sleep in the rooms inside the East Tower, they claim they never get a decent nights sleep due to the paranormal phenomena that occur. If you are sat on the bottom step reading this book you are where the ghosts like to be. Often when you are in the rooms you can hear people coming up and down the stairs and walking along the corridor, you can even see them sometimes when you are in the oubliette room. You may see light or feet walking along, going past the bedroom, glimpsed through the tiny gap under the door.

Teachers often report the sound of children running up and down the stairs and laughter coming from the tower. When they sneak in quietly to catch them they realise there is no one there, not only are there no naughty children running around but they are actually all tucked up asleep in their beds. Other groups have made complaints to the management in the mornings about how noisy the children in the East Tower were, only to be told that there were no children staying in the Tower, or even better no children staying in the entire castle.

Running water, Automatic Lights

Keep your ears open when sat here, and not only might you hear the children, but be aware that the ghosts like to wash their hands after using the facilities. Taps have been known to turn themselves on and off in the toilets and showers in the East Tower. Of course the sceptics will tell us that it's something to do with the plumbing in an old building, that may be so, but it can be very unnerving standing there watching a tap slowly turn itself on after you have used the toilet, in fact it often makes you want to use the toilet again.

Another thing that obviously could be down to faulty or aging workmanship are the lights. I have often turned the lights off on a 'Ghost Night' evening only to come along five minutes later and someone or something has turned them all back on again. This normally happens in the corridors, and not in the bedrooms. The average person would think it is not paranormal and that someone must have just turned them all back on again, but you have to remember that during a 'Ghost Night' we account for where everyone is, and we know that the tower has been empty and when we return to it, not only have the lights turned on, but the light switches have moved into different positions meaning it is not a wiring fault, but a physical movement that has happened.

The Oubliette

"What is an oubliette?" I hear you ask, or if you have been on one of the Ghost Nights at the castle, you may have overheard other people asking.

"What is an Oubilydoubily?", or the more popular "What is an Oublythingy?"

Well people will know what it is if they have watched the greatest film in the world, Jim Henson's 'Labyrinth',(I know that is subjective but I would like to point out that I am correct, Labyrinth is an amazing film and Jim Henson is Godlike for making it). If you have not watched this epic then I may need to explain, the word itself comes from the French word - To Forget, because if you went into this room that is what is supposed to happen to you. You were forgotten about, until you died.

Let me explain, head into the room if it is open, and may I suggest sitting on the bed that is in the first window alcove on the right as you walk through the door. Sit facing the room and often on the floor we have a large rug, in front of the heater. This is not because it is such a lovely warm inviting room that you may wish to curl up on a rug and fall asleep, far from it. The rug normally covers the trap door leading to the Oubliette itself.

Under the floor of this room is a large cavernous dungeon, a cell where there is only one way in, and technically no way out. If you lift the trap door and look inside be very careful, because we mean it when we say there is no way out. If something falls out of your pocket into the pit it stays there. Someone from English heritage eventually comes along and fishes things out every few years or so, hence our collection of broken mobile phones that have jumped out of peoples shirt pockets. The castle has been used for many things in it's past but the most gruesome have to be the times when it was used as a place of incarceration and execution. If you were lucky then the East Towers prison was possibly one of the better places to be, if you were ever thrown into an Oubliette then you had better hope that you were thrown head first and died from the impact.

People have been known to survive for years in oubliettes as jailers might throw them food from time to time, and some castles would use the prisoners as a waste disposal unit and throw any waste products into the cell for them to eat. The other way people have been known to survive was by either eating the occasional unfortunate rat that fell or wandered in or even worse by eating each other. The first to die in a group of prisoners was very likely to also be the first course.

So now you know what this room may have been used for, let me give you a few words of hope, especially if you are sleeping in this room. The hole in the floor may have also been used as some form of store room, and not actually had cannibalistic prisoners in it at all. It is up to you to decide which tale you prefer if you want a decent nights sleep.

I do hope that you are sat on the bed that we have recommended as this is where I will start our first tale of spookiness, I do apologise if you are sleeping in this bed, but there is not much we can do about this ghost, I think that it was a resident long before you were here, and may have some form of spooky squatters rights.

The Scary Bed

If you are sleeping in this bed, then already we are not off to a good start with a title like that are we. But it is true this is possibly the scariest place to sleep in the entire castle. Most of the ghosts we have here are harmless little phantoms that will wander around ignoring you, a few may poke and prod you from time to time, but this one is possibly the most disturbing of them all.

Saying all this if you are a sceptical ghost hunter, then perhaps this is the bed to sleep in to try and turn you into a believer, for it is in this bed that guest report being woken up in the night, by an angry ghost. It seems to feel as though you should not be there, because it tries to steal the sheets from you. How stereotypical a ghost is this? it wants to steal your sheets, possibly to put over itself and wander around making strange WOOOO! noises. I should not treat this story too lightly, as it seems to be the one that scares people the most.

The Scary Bed on the right

One lady was found in tears one morning after spending the night in this room, she was not actually in this room crying but in the King John's Lounge instead.

The Oubliette room as seen from the moat, the window in the bottom left corner is where the 'Scary Bed' is situated

She told the castle that there was no way that she was going back into the room, not even to pack her things. When questioned about why she was so upset, she said that she could not cope with the noise of the screaming woman. This is a noise that is often reported by people sleeping in this bed. You must also be aware of the work that various paranormal groups have done in this room, and that the acoustics in this window alcove are rather unusual. If you lay down with your head at the window end of the bed, you will notice the strange echo type sound, as the noises bounce around the window alcove. Noises from outside can become amplified in this area, and noises can be heard whilst sat here that no one else in the room can hear.

We take into consideration all these elements when people tell us about screaming women, and we also tell them that perhaps they heard a fox outside. This may seem strange but if you are not from around the countryside some noises can be very disturbing, and I have on more than one occasion run out into the grounds because of a screaming noise to see a screeching owl flying off into the distance. So with all these possibilities in mind we talk to the guests who have experienced these things, and it seems that the noise emanates from inside the room.

As well as the screaming, heavy distressed breathing can be heard as though it is right next to your ear, and sometimes you can even feel the breath on your face. The woman in our story was scared enough by the screaming lady, but the thing that sent her petrified running from the room, was that as she lay there, the sheets were ripped off the bed as though by some invisible hand.

This is a story repeated several times by guests sleeping in this bed, sometimes, people are booked in for several days and get so scared they leave after one night. Sometimes they do not even wait until the morning, one such incident was when two cyclists were staying for several days, and during the first night, they left very early in the morning, apparently leaving some excuse about the sheets moving by themselves. My favourite story is about a man that is most definitely braver than me. When the staff went into the room in the morning they asked him why he had moved the bed up against one of the walls. His reply was that it was the only way that he could get the sheets to stopped being pulled off him in the night, he was the only person in the room, and at no point thought that this was too scary for him. Personally I would have been out of the room in a split second, dedicated ghost hunter that I am, I am most definitely not brave enough to lay there waiting to see if I am the next thing to be thrown off the bed.

One woman claims that she was 'touched on the bum', whist lying on the scary bed, this had happened twice. During the night there were two people (mother and daughter) staying in that room, they both got rather scared and decided to both sleep in the bed, but instead of sleeping in another bed they both slept in the scary bed.

During the remainder of the evening they both experienced being touched or grabbed by unseen hands. Obviously they checked that it was not the other person in the bed, and every time there was no rational explanation for these groping encounters.

They also both heard something breathing heavily very close to them. The obvious thing that anyone reading this would say is that as they were sleeping in the same bed they must have accidentally breathed in each others ear, or touched the other person somehow, yet when this hypothesis was raised they both said that they knew where the other person was, and they had obviously reasoned this themselves.

The Fluctuating Temperature

It seems that there is an ongoing argument between the spirits in the room as to what temperature they would like it, an afterlife struggle over a thermostat. Not the most exciting ghost in the castle, but to ghost hunters this is a measurable phenomena. One of the ghost hunting groups that I belong to have been running an ongoing experiment for many years now at the castle collecting data and readings throughout the castle. This room always gives us the most interesting temperature fluctuations.

I would like to point out to fellow ghost hunters that many locations will give temperature readings that seem unusual and go up and down, but not like this room. My favourite example of this is when I was holding two thermometers and my colleague was holding another one about 3 feet away from me, my arms were outstretched so that the thermometers that I had were about two foot apart. All three thermometers showed different temperatures. This fact in itself is not unusual as often thermometers are not calibrated that well, but the differences between the three were enormous, One showed 7 degrees Celsius another about 14 and the third about 21 degrees.

Don't you open that trapdoor because there's something down there

Before you start thinking that this ghost was trying to tell us that it could do its seven times table, I would like to point out that these temperature readings can happen rapidly, every few seconds the readings would drop or rise, sometimes by as much as 10 degrees over the space of thirty seconds. This carried on for about ten or fifteen minutes, before it stopped completely and all three then showed approximately the same temperature. I will point out that there were not heat sources in the room, and no major draughts. The castle obviously has heating issues due to the nature of the building, but these were all accounted for, leaving us with no rational explanation. Our group are not the only group that come and stay at the castle and this phenomena has been reported, albeit not as drastically as this, on many occasions.

BOLS

An unusual thing to type, or say, I grant you that. It actually stands for Ball Of Light. Over the years many people have got very excited about small white lights that appear on night vision cameras. Many mediums and psychics claim that these are the first stages of a physical manifestation of a ghost or spirit, personally I would say that ninety nine percent of these are dust and insects not within the focal range of the lens. People are perfectly entitled to their own opinions, but even the camera manufacturers have admitted this now. Some however seem to defy this explanation, and this castle is full of them.

The best type of BOL is one that can be seen with the naked eye, we have managed to get some great footage of these types, in shot you often see people pointing to where they can see the BOLS, and these are not just small flickers of possible dust we have seen some bright glowing objects about the size of footballs appearing on camera, and in view with the naked eye.

The nature of the BOL's in the castle are different depending on which room you are in, and often have different colours to them, in this room they tend to be white or blue, and are sometimes seen rising out of the trap door area. In other rooms the colours can vary, and we will mention them as we guide you around the building.

The Ghost That Likes To Stroke

Well done if you are in a group and have managed to avoid getting the scary bed; but do not be so quick to relax, as there is another bed that has rather unpleasant paranormal associations. The bed that is immediately on your left as you walk into the room, is often a bunk bed, (I say often as the castle staff occasionally rearrange the rooms and furniture) People who have slept in this bed, have reported being touched and stroked, so I guess for some people this may be the best bed to stay in depends on your outlook. Various colleagues of mine have experienced it, and said it is not too pleasant, it feels like an arm brushing over the top of you.

I was sleeping in this room, and a fellow ghost hunter by the name of Bruce was lying in this bed, and I was in one opposite, I was woken up by a loud thudding noise of something hitting the floor. We were both shaken and startled, and in our newly awakened state we finally deduced that it was the phone that was lying on the floor near Bruce's bed. Just as we were both about to slip back into our sleepy heads, we both sat up and asked each other why had the phone landed on the floor.

Neither of us could remember seeing it in some precarious place, and looking around us there was no evidence of either of us sleep walking and knocking something over. So for the first time in ages I got out of bed very early and went for breakfast, Bruce did exactly the same as neither of us wanted to be left in the room on our own.

I have recently been told by some ghost hunters that stayed over that one of their throng was asleep and felt as if their partner had got onto the bed and was holding them. They spoke to their partner, and did not get a reply which they considered odd, so they asked the question again, and still no reply. The ghost hunter thought that their partner was just being rude so moved and felt the other person let go of them, as they sat up they realised there was no one else in the room. This was closely followed by them not being in the room as well.

If You're Happy And You Know It Clap Your Hands

One of my fellow ghost hunting colleagues that has visited this castle a lot is Dave, I value his opinion a great deal when it comes to hauntings here, as he has visited the building so often. Familiarity with these premises is a great asset when it comes to ascertaining which are regular noises and the things that go bump in the night. This noise however was not a regular 'Bump In The Night'.

Dave was stood in the oubliette room, and about 4 or 5 foot away from him was another guest, they said that in between them a loud single clap was heard. Dave thought that it may well have been a laminated A4 map of the castle that was blue tacked to the back of the door falling down. No one saw this happen however, and even he said it sounded like it was three dimensionally between him and this other ghost hunter. This same group also heard someone walk down the stairs and along the corridor and past by the Oubliette door, it was not until afterwards that we ascertained that this was not possible as there was no one else in that part of the castle and that everyone was accounted for.

Disembodied Voices

I always feel the term 'Disembodied Voices' sounds a lot more sinister than it actually is. What we mean is the sound of a conversation when there is no one there to make the noise. I have found that these experiences can often be very disturbing, as you can hear someone say something, and even work out where the noise emanated from yet there is no one stood there. Even worse is when you hear these noises on your own, as you have to think, "now was that a Ghost, or have I finally gone mad,". So putting aside the possibility of men in white coats taking you to a lovely place with padded cells, let us assume that these voices are in some way paranormal. I use the term paranormal here to mean something not normal, not necessarily a visit from your dead aunty Marie telling you to feed the cats.

The first time I walked into the castle was to film a program where we were providing the ghost hunting element, a light hearted piece all about spooks and freak goings on in the night. I have done countless things like this for newspapers, TV, radio, and magazines, and each time we do it becomes more and more annoying, they never seem to actually listen, and no matter how many times you tell them to take it seriously they always seem to turn it into some light comedy piece at the end of the local news. Well we were here thinking it was going to be exactly the same as any other piece of Halloween entertainment, but we were gladly mistaken.

Paul from the paranormal group Parasoc and I were told that it would be a while before we were filming so we took the opportunity to wander around and do a spot of filming ourselves. We headed into the East Tower and stood outside the door of the Oubliette room. We wanted to come into the room and film some things for ourselves but, as we were about to open the door we heard a conversation inside the room, not knowing this was a bedroom, we thought it must be an office of some description. Rather than disturb the people in the office we thought we would film elsewhere and come back to this room when it was less busy. Heading upstairs into the Constables room, and the Chaplains room we didn't get much of a sense of how haunted the place was, but looked forward to filming here. When we returned back downstairs we could not hear any voices in the Oubliette room, so we knocked on the door and tried to walk in. The door was locked, and there was no noise coming from inside this time, so we headed back to the office to get the key from the castle manager, who was in the West Tower.

When we asked for the key to the Oubliette room we were told that it had not been opened all day, we insisted that it must have been as we had heard the voices from inside. The manager then produced the key and said no one had unlocked the door all day, and the whereabouts of everyone that was in the castle had been accounted for. Paul and I were quite impressed that in our first ten minutes of being here we had experienced something possibly paranormal. More importantly like a lot of the ghosts and paranormal activity in this building it was so real that we just accepted that it must have been real people.

Rattling Chains and Padlocks

The stereotypical ghost if it is not a large sheet with eye holes cut into it, will hopefully wail and make, "OOOO!" noises, but more importantly it should rattle chains for some reason. Well the ghost in the Oubliette does the next best thing, it rattles a padlock. If the Oubliette trapdoor is open then please look into it and see the large metal padlock that holds the grill shut. During the evening that has been heard, and seen to move of its own accord. Some people will say it is the heating and cooling of the building at night that makes all these strange noises, and the contraction of the metal obviously is to blame when the padlock makes a noise. Well this explanation would be a good one, if it were not for the fact that several people have seen the padlock moving for several seconds, and even get lifted up, and shaken violently.

Mary and Elizabeth

Before you get excited this castle may have royal connections but we are not talking about the Mary and Elizabeth of monarchical fame here, no it transpires that these may have been servants. When I do investigations of haunted buildings I tend to stick to what can be proven, and facts. Other groups can come into buildings with mediums, they hold séances, they do Ouija boards, and various other methods of possibly communicating with the dead. When this happens the two names that come up again, and again are Mary and Elizabeth, who are supposedly both servant girls.

Unfortunately these are such common names that at some point in this castles history I am positive there have been servants by the name of Elizabeth or Mary. One thing I will add though is that time and time again the mediums, and séances give Mary's age at around 14 years old, and that she worked here, but did not live in the castle. The sad side to this tale is that at least fifty percent of the time the story given to these ghosts is that one of them was sexually attacked by someone who lived at the castle, so perhaps she is the source of the female screams that are heard so often in this room.

The Footsteps

One of the most common haunting in the castle have to be the footsteps, the ghosts in this castle wander all over the place, and can be heard to do so. We have made many recordings on our Ghost Nights, and one of the best has to have come from this room. Unfortunately we have not captured the sound of the screaming, or of the children playing and running around, but we have recorded the sound of footsteps and of furniture being dragged around.

It is quite common for us to lock a room with a camera or a digital recorder of some sort running inside it. When we return we can guarantee that no one has been in that room as we have the key in our hands. This allows us to continue an investigation even when we do not have enough people to cover the whole castle. One such recording is about 10 minutes of someone pacing around with heavy boots on the wooden floor, the sound is sometimes punctuated with what sounds like one of the stools being moved across the floor, the recording ends with Emma (another ghost hunting colleague) walking through the door walking over to the recorder and turning it off. She can definitely verify that there was no one else in the room when she walked in. We have done extensive experiments to see if the noise could have been from another room and somehow travelled to this one, and the only thing that came close to the noise was one of our investigators walking heavily around in the Oubliette room, and dragging stools around.

Another example of the footstep noises that can be heard quite clearly seem to be upstairs, if you are stood in the Oubliette room, even if there is no one else in the castle you may get to hear people walking around upstairs, this has been reported to us many times. During the Ghost Nights at the castle we have often had groups complaining that their ghost hunting vigil was ruined by whichever group was upstairs in the Constable's room walking around and moving too much. It is always interesting to see how long it takes them to believe you when you tell them that they were the only people in that tower, they will stand adamantly protesting that you are wrong. We have had to question everyone about their whereabouts before just to be able to ascertain that the footsteps must be of paranormal origin.

The Dark Shadow

There are several dark shadowy figures that get seen around the castle, now whether it is one spirit that likes to wander or whether it is a collection of ghosts throughout the building we do not know. The one that is seen in this room tends to be spotted near the fireplace. Yet again we have done numerous experiments with lights shining through windows, creating shadows, and turning lights on and off throughout the building, and nothing we have tried can seem to create the same image of the dark figure.

Under the Doorway

Do not forget that if you see someone walk past the door always go out into the corridor and check to see if it is a real person, especially if it looks like a small pair of feet, or you hear the sound of children.

Many groups have sat in this room and see what looks like people walking past the door, normally down the stairs and out into the gatehouse. People have also heard the sound of others walking through the gatehouse, and main doors, only to find out that there is not only no one there, but that the main castle doors have been bolted so that there is no possible way that anyone could have walked out of the main gate.

Whilst sat in the room, people have heard horses trot along on the stones outside the fire exit, and through the main gates. A noise that we will later learn has been heard in other parts of the castle. Thankfully due to the technical nature of ghost hunting we have often had cameras, or witnesses situated in places that can prove that there has not been anyone in the places that these noises have been heard emanating from.

The view from the Oubliette room window

Chapter 2 - The East Tower
The Constables Room

We now head out of the Oubliette room, and up the stairs to the next floor. As you go up the stairs and round the corner you will see a door in front of you, and a steep staircase off to the left. The stairs lead to the Chaplain's room, but let us not concern ourselves with this room just yet, instead head into the Constable's room.

I will tell you that these are not the original stairs, which would account for the fact that to door opens out onto a staircase and not a flat landing area, please be aware of this when you come back out of the room, as we don't want you falling down the stairs, and adding another ghost to the tower.

In this room we still get reports of the sound of children and footsteps on the stairs, but we also get reports of the BOL's (Balls Of Light) and the one in this room is of particular interest, if you sit on the bed in the second window alcove you may get to see it.

The BOL

As we have said the BOL's in the castle can be different colours and the one in this room is always white. The most intriguing thing about this BOL is that it always seems to travel along the same path. People sat on the beds have said that they see a small ball appear in the middle of the floor and float towards the fire exit where it disappears again.

During one of the ghost hunting nights one person turned around to see the BOL in the middle of the floor, and as they had not seen it appear they assumed it must have been there all along, she even bent down to pick it up thinking it was a ball on the floor somehow reflecting some light from somewhere, as she did bend down the BOL moved towards the door and disappeared. As we mentioned earlier a lot of the paranormal activity in this castle is so realistic that people do not question it, and if she had not bent down to pick up the BOL, then perhaps se may have walked out of the room thinking that nothing unusual had happened.

Attack of the Ghostly Lurgy

One thing I have always said is that ghosts are harmless and cannot do anything to you that should cause you alarm. Here is where I may possibly be wrong. When things do happen in this room they can be quite disturbing. Most of the time the only warning you need about ghosts is that you should not run away from them, not for any weird reason that they may chase you, but more because you are in an old building with worn steps and dark corridors and you may end up falling down stairs or banging your head on the low ceilings.

So when a ghost phsyically affects people it can be very interesting for us to investigate. In this room we have had reports of people feeling faint, others being sick, and worst of all the sensation of being choked or strangled. There are also weird smells that emanate from this room, and I don't mean from tired ghost hunters that have had a day of eating baked beans, the strange thing about these smells is often they stop as soon as you walk out of the room. That does not mean that you were the person responsible for the smell, what I mean is if you walk out, and then turn around and go straight back in the smell has stopped. What is unusual is that the putrid smell can be very strong for about five seconds and then completely disappear. Sometimes the luckier ghost hunters get the smell of flowers suddenly waft through the room.

I am well aware of the psychological effects of mass hysteria, and some of these incidents may be put down to this, and this explanation may go to explain some of the phantoms and paranormal activity throughout the building, but we normally only get these stories from this room. Personal responses to haunting can always be described as mass hysteria or delusion, and I have met many delusional ghost hunters in my time, but it is a lot harder to explain away something physical that can be registered by more than one person, so smells, lights, figures and shapes, are always more interesting for us to examine.

Noisy Doors

We have a few doors in the castle that seem to have a mind of their own, this room has one such door. Anyone that has spent a great deal of time in this room will tell you that the door is not a perfect seal and has been known to move in the wind. Even though it is a quite still evening the slightest breeze or even someone opening a door somewhere else in the tower can cause this door to move slightly. Some groups have got very excited thinking that they are witnessing something paranormal when in reality it is basic physics.

Having said all that this door can suddenly fly open, with no one stood either side of it, and no visible means of propulsion. One ghost hunting group claims to have used this door to communicate with some form of spirit. They would ask questions and if it was a "yes" answer the door would open. They claim that the door opened quite a distance and not just swung in the breeze.

As well as the moving doors, we have a ghost that likes to move furniture, and one ghost seems to focus on moving beds. We have had strange reports of one bed that seemed to vibrate , it appeared to shake when there was no one stood near it. A few groups that have seen this have made sure that they did not even move so that it could not be caused by some ill fitting floorboard that someone had stood on, and yet the bed continued to move.

A Shaky Bed

The middle bed on the left hand side when you walk into the room, has been seen by two different ghost hunting groups to move of its own accord. The description that both groups have given on separate nights was that the bed started shaking very slightly and if you put your hand onto it you could feel it vibrate, the bed would then eventually move a slight amount and stop abruptly.

Ghost Rustlers

During one ghost hunting evening back in 2009 we first encountered our ghost rustler. I do not mean someone that surreptitiously sneaks in a removes our ghosts with a lasso, whilst on horseback. No this is a ghostly noise, it is the sound of rustling coming from near one of the beds. Each time the noise was heard it was checked out but to no avail, nothing was ever found to account for the noise.

We did all the obvious things like checking for paper and a breeze, or even holes for mice to come through, we even set up cameras for days trying to find out whether a mouse was responsible for the noises, but to no avail. The noise has returned on many occasions but each time we can never work out what is causing it.

The remains of the East Tower on the same floor as the Constables Room

Chapter 3 - The East Tower
The Chaplains Room

As you walk out of the room be careful, as we have already mentioned the door opens out onto a staircase, now turn left and head up the stairs. Yet another warning here as well, the ceiling is low and the stairs are steep so please be careful. When you walk into the Chaplain's room you will see a low ceiling and a room full of beds, on the far wall you will see a fire exit, please do not open these fire exits throughout the castle, as they will set off the fire alarms. In the middle of the ceiling you may also see a hatch, please do not open this either. There are often bats up there, and the only thing you may be investigating is the shower room as you are trying to wash off the bat poo that will fall on your head. We also tell people that if you hear strange scratching noises it may well be the bats in the attic, as some ghost groups have reported this noise in this room.

A very rare view of the church taken from the battlements that are not accessible to the public. The Chaplains room roof is visible on the right and the hanging room on the left.

More Footsteps

We have one of our rather energetic ghosts in this room, they seem to get a lot of exercise as they walk around the castle. I was in the Constable's room below this one, and doing a recording for a radio show. As I was recording I commentated on the fact that I could hear someone walking around in the Chaplain's room, as though they were near the windows that face out towards the graveyard. I assumed that the person walking around was another ghost hunter that happened to be up there videoing and recording as well.

Once the interview was over I went upstairs to see if the ghost hunter had experienced anything, she claimed that she had not seen anything, but had heard footsteps in exactly the place that I had heard them, she however had sat perfectly still at the far end of the room next to the door at the top of the stairs. She had even had the video camera running and could prove that she had not moved at all.

This room has more beds than most, which just means when something happens we get more witnesses

The Dark Figures

Most paranormal happenings and haunting are very mundane, or sometimes barely even noticeable. There will be footsteps walking in corridors, that unless you can account for everyone in the castle you would probably ignore assuming it was someone else in the castle. There may be lights that you assume are someone else's torch, or cars going passed a window and headlights flashing against the wall. We do take all these into account, and if we can create the same effect via normal methods then we tend to ignore them. We only write down the tales that have happened several times to different witnesses that are highly unlikely to have corroborated on a fanciful tale. We also include stories from the castle staff as they are used to all the strange noises, and shadows that the castle creates.

Two members of staff from the castle have told me of figures that they have seen in the Chaplain's room, and when I did a bit more research it seems as though others have seen these figures in the past. The problem with these ghosts, if you are easily scared, is that they stand in front of the door, so I am afraid you will have to ask them to move out of the way before you run screaming out of the room and down the stairs.

The Flasher

Do not get too excited this is not what it sounds like, there are many strange lights throughout the castle as we have explained about when we talked of BOL's. The lights in this room can be slightly different.

I must point out that the way the eye works can create strange lights and sparks especially when in low light conditions, so to the sceptics out there I would like to point out that we have taken all of that into consideration and the stories of BOL's and flashing lights in the castle are highly unlikely to caused by this effect.

On one ghost hunting night we had about eight people doing a ghost hunting vigil in this room, and they had decided to turn off the lights. I now need to explain one of the rules of ghost hunting, if you are planning on using a camera with a flash, you should always say the word "FLASH" before you take photograph. If you do not warn others that you are about to take a photo, then you will have a room of very angry ghost hunters all of which are seeing spots before their eyes, as they have lost their night vision because of your camera flash. One evening these ghost hunters were all getting annoyed as someone was taking photo's and not saying flash, obviously being British no one wanted to say anything, apart from the occasional 'Tut' registering their annoyance. Eventually someone had had enough, and got up and turned the rooms light on to admonish the perpetrator of this foul crime. When the lights came on they realised that no one in the room actually had a camera, and where the few flashes had come from, no one was even sat there.

The other BOL's in this room tend to be red in colour, and are often seen near the beds closest to the fire exit.

The Ghost That Likes To Stroke Part Two

The previous group of ghost hunters that experienced the Flasher also experienced the ghost that likes to touch you. They seemed to get a lot of paranormal activity that night, and as per usual which ever room is the one that has the most activity will be the opposite side to the castle where we have set up all the cameras and equipment. Unlike other haunted buildings that have one or two haunted rooms, the entire castle is populated by many phantoms, and so it makes it difficult to predict where will be the most likely place for paranormal activity.

On many ghost hunts we have set up an array of cameras and monitors only to have the phenomena happen directly behind us and out of shot. On this particular evening we had set up most of our recording devices in the West Tower due to the fact that the previous ghost hunt had so many things happen over in that tower that we decided to try and catch it on tape.

On this particular evening one of the ghost hunters said that she had felt something stroking her neck and kept touching her head, this happened over a period of about 5 minutes. There are natural things that can occur to the body that can give you this sensation, it often feels like someone brushing over the top of your hair. When these types of phenomena occur we often just ignore it, yet the reason I note it in this mighty tome is because it always seems to occur in the Chaplain's room. Yes you may get other instances of it in other places, but about 90 percent of the time it is in this room. The ghost hunter who reported this to me, seemed to think she was being silly and it was not until I showed her the copious amounts of entries in my records books from all the people who had reported it previously that she became upset.

The Affluent Ghost

Ghost hunting is a very expensive hobby, and a set of night vision cameras, a thermal imaging unit, EMF meters, Laptops, Microphones, and digital recorders can easily set you back thousands of pounds, and I think the thing you get through the most is coffee, chocolate, and batteries. So with all these expenses in mind then you may want to stay in the Chaplain's room, as this ghost likes to give a refund.

One group were in this room on a ghost hunting vigil, and decided to do a thing called calling out. "Calling Out" is where instead of sitting quietly in a room waiting for something to happen you try and provoke the ghost into a reaction. This does not mean you have to make the ghost angry, and call it names, or make snide comments about doubting its ectoplasmic capabilities, instead it means you can ask a question and try and get some form of response.

The response vary depending on the phantom, sometimes you may hear a knocking noise, sometimes the lights may go on and off, the theory being that the ghost has in some way learned to manipulate that piece of equipment or its environment. This group were calling out trying to get a response, when a coin rolled over towards them, it was a large old Penny. We were understandably sceptical about the whole situation and thought that one of them had perhaps rolled the coin slyly along the floor as a joke. We voiced our doubts, to be met with a unified response saying that not only was it not them that had done it, but also the coin had come from an area that no one was sitting in, so it could not possibly have been any of them.

My dad collects old coins so was naturally interested in the year and type of coin, so any other of you coin collectors out there, I am afraid to say it was not too interesting a specimen. It was an 1891 penny and as yet I have not come across anything interesting that happened in that year at the castle. Feel free to email me if you manage to find out there was a murder of the castle's treasurer in that year.

The Bed Mover

The castle has various rooms of various sizes, and if you are actually in the room reading this book you will know that this is one of the larger dorms with twelve beds in it. That does not always mean that twelve people always sleep in here, as often there is less, but sometimes there is more. People have reported being in bed, just lying there, or sitting quietly and something gets in next to them. This can happen in the middle of the day or with the lights on so they know full well there is not actually anybody there, yet they have claimed to see the bed move or the mattress depress down as though someone is sat there.

Not only does it sit down next to you, but it can also move the bed, even when there are people on it. One Ghost Hunting night we saw three people come down the stairs rather perturbed as they were all sat on one bed and it was moved about three inches or more, none of them had their feet on the floor, or were leaning against it to make it move either.

If it does not move the bed, it may actually move the floor, and groups have witnessed the floor physically vibrating, and you can feel it through your shoes, or if you place your hand on the floor.

The Twitching Curtain

Strange noises come from this room on regular occasions, we have phantom footsteps, we have voices, vibrating floors, and so on, but a more unusual one is the sound of the curtains being opened. This haunting occurs in other parts of the castle as well, but is predominantly heard in this room. It is heard in the state apartments, and also the guard room, but here the noise happens and when you turn around you notice the curtains are open. We have never managed to be there at the right time with a camera pointing in the right direction, but this is one that I desperately want to capture on video, as it proves that ghosts can move things.

I personally have no doubt what so ever that ghosts are capable of moving things as I have experienced several poltergeist throughout my ghost hunting years, and later in this book we will tell you all about our resident poltergeist.

The Talking Man

A few guests were staying in this room one night, and they were the only ones still awake in their family their father was lying on a bed on the other side of the room, and they thought he was talking, nothing interesting in fact they assumed that there were two other people (including their father) on the other side of the room chatting. They later found out that there was not anyone other than their father, so even if we discount the fact that he was talking in his sleep, then who was the voice that was replying to him.

Get Out Of Bed

We have a few ghosts in the castle that can move things, these are normally known as Poltergeists, from the German phrase meaning 'noisy ghost'. Poltergeists are disturbing when they move things around but even more disturbing when they try to move you.

One guest told me a tale that illustrates this perfectly in this room, she was dozing off trying to sleep, and she felt as though she had been pushed towards the wall. I asked her if it could possibly have been that she was half asleep and just fell out of bed and it made her think she had been pushed.

The windows from the bottom up are the oubliette, then the constables room, then the chaplains on the top floor

She told me that could not be the case as she didn't fall out of bed instead it felt like a hand pushing her against the wall when she was in bed, as though it was someone trying to shake her and make sure she was awake. The obvious thing is to think that she was actually being pushed by someone in the room, yet the only other people in the room were already asleep and on the other side to where she was trying to sleep.

After she felt the push, she heard voices, she said it was like someone saying, 'Oi!' which made her feel that this thing did not want her to sleep. Then there was some loud talking, and then whispers. She was adamant that there was no one else in the room that was awake, and that these voices did not come from the direction of where the other sleepers were.

Warm Breath

I have had a few descriptions of touching, pushing, and noises in this room, but another regular haunting throughout the castle is the heavy breather. In this room I have had a few reports where it feels like someone stood next to you and breathing into your ear. It is not just the noise of breathing, you can actually feel the warm breath on your face.

Be careful as you head out the room as the ceiling is very low on the way down the stairs and you could hit your head, also be aware of the steep stair case, and hold onto the rails as you descend. As we have mentioned before the original staircase is no longer in this tower as it was where the drying room now is, and you can still see the circular nature of that part of the building from inside that room, or by standing on tip toe in the guard house and looking over the roof towards the back left corner.

We are now going to continue our tour of the castle by heading back through the main door next to the office, and turning left. You should now be stood in the old kitchen with a large wooden staircase on your left. Walk all the way to the top of these stairs, and the next flight of stairs on the next floor, this should take us all the way up to the Hanging room and Guard Room

Look out for the ghosts running up and down the stairs on your way out of the east tower. For the technical ghost hunters out there you will notice the fuse boxes which can make for some strange readings on your ghost hunting equipment.

Chapter 4 - The West Tower
The Hanging Room and the Guard Room

The hanging room window is in the top right hand corner

As you walk into the Guard room, you will see a large mirror on the left hand side, take note of this as we will be returning to this later, and getting you to try the parapsychology experiment called scrying. There will be a window alcove in front of you, and to the right of the door you will see a window. It is a good idea to have a look around you and see if any of the windows or curtains are open, this will make sense later on. Also take a look out of the window to the right of the door and see out into what was once part of the guardhouse, as you look across to the East Tower.

I suggest sitting in the window alcove, on one of the small stools if you can find one, make yourself comfortable and before you read on, try calling out to see if you can get any of the ghosts to join you whilst you are sat there.

The Screaming Man

I included this story as I thought it may be of interest to show how someone being scared can set off a night of hysteria in others. The basics of the tale are as follows, six people were sleeping in the Guard room, and one man had a nightmare and screamed his head off, he managed whilst thrashing around to cut himself and get blood everywhere. When the rest of the castle wakes up to hear this they see a man screaming with blood on him, at which point rumours and stories are rife through the castle and everyone is on edge for the rest of the night.

The interesting part of the story when we delved deeper into it however was that one of our Ghost hunters, by the name of Dave was also sleeping in that room. He said that for about ten minutes before this happened, he heard a strange noise, like a humming, buzzing, and scuttling noise going across the ceiling and when it finally settled directly above the man in question, that was when the man awoke screaming. So perhaps something made the man have the nightmare after all.

The Figure in the Doorway

Yet again we see our dark figures in the castle, this one however seems to be slightly more solid than the others, very often people will talk about a shadow, or a shadowy figure, something that does not seem to have much substance to it. This figure however often seems to appear like a solid entity, but still like a dark shadow at the same time.

The doorway that so many guests have seen a figure standing in

Many people, including myself, have seen this figure stood in the doorway between the guard room and the hanging room. I saw a figure that seemed to have no features on its face, and after a few seconds just dissolved and faded away.

Many people have also witnessed this dark creature, other people describe him as a silhouette, which dissolves seconds after you look at him. It does seem to be described as a 'He', which is strange as the other figure that is seen in this area of the castle is a woman, but I shall come onto the subject of her very shortly.

People describe the sensation of this thing being malevolent and staring at them, a lot of people think that these rooms are the most unpleasant, myself included. Dave (a fellow ghost hunter) and I once stayed at the castle and the only room we had free was the guard room, we decided that we would rather sleep on the sofas in the Old Kitchen instead, as this room scared us so much.

This figure has been seen reflected in the mirror by various people, and when they turn startled expecting someone to be stood there, there is no one. When they turn around to look in the mirror again the figure has gone.

Possibly the scariest figure you could ever see in a mirror one of the castle staff, this time its Neil taking one of the many pictures he contributed to this book.

Marbles

Perhaps these ghosts just like playing with us, and the next one definitely sounds like he does. People have reported what sounds like marbles being dropped or rolled along the floor, yet there is never anything to see when you look. This has been witnessed by several people at the same time, making it unlikely to be an auditory hallucination.

EMF results

There is a piece of ghost hunting equipment called an EMF meter, this measures the electro magnetic field, (or Frequency) that is in the atmosphere. If held next to a television, or stereo they will give off high readings. It is thought in some circles that thee pieces of kit can be used to measure ghosts. Let me get one thing straight though, they are not ghost detectors before you all rush off to eBay and start spending lots of hard earned pennies, all they do is measure the field.

One theory is that a high electro magnetic field can cause the brain to hallucinate, and can alter the way you think, it has even been blamed in some cases of poltergeist activity. So what some people think of as a ghost detector may actually only be something to measure the possibility of delusions.

Having said all that I will tell you about another phenomena called Orbs. I need to briefly explain what all these things are, to be able to explain this next story. An orb some people think is the first manifestation of a ghost and they are generally seen as small white lights seen on night vision cameras. Most people now assume that these are dust particles or insects too close to the lens therefore not allowing the auto focus to pick them up properly. The way that night vision works is that an infra red beam comes out from the camera and bounces off objects so that the camera can film them. When a dust particle is close to the lens this can reflect and flare creating what looks like a large white Orb on the screen.

Now when we filmed in the Guard room, one of our colleagues was using an EMF meter and all of a sudden we got an Orb on the screen of the video camera, we did not think too much of it, until it floated towards the ghost hunter with the EMF meter. The meter then seemed to register a small reading as this thing flew over the top of it. This may not seem much to someone who is not a ghost hunter, but to parapsychologists this is gold dust.

The Pusher

Let us get away from these boring technical ghost tales, and back to the spooky stuff instead. I have experienced one of the reoccurring ghosties in the Guard room, and if you are stood or sat in the window alcove then hopefully you will too.

I was stood with a group in the Guard room who were all doing a parapsychological experiment called scrying. Whilst the group were all staring into a mirror hoping that ghosties would start staring back at them, I felt something push into my back and made me take a few steps.

It felt as though someone had placed their hand on my back and just pushed, not particularly hard, but hard enough to put me off balance. I naturally turned around, yet there was no one behind me. I did not tell anyone what had just happened, and decided to keep this story to myself until later.

About five minutes later this happened to a woman that had moved to where I was stood. I stupidly forgot to write it down that it had happened to me. The reason you should always write things down like this as they occur is that now if I said , "Oh yes that happened to me as well" no one would believe me.

If this is currently your view then beware you may be attacked by the pushing ghost

We are not the only two people to get pushed in this way, and several ghost hunters that I trust implicitly have been pushed whilst stood here, and I have witnessed a woman get pushed so hard as she was walking towards the doorway between the rooms, that she went flying backwards and knocked over the metal cover on the radiators.

The Ghost That Likes To Stroke Part Three

A friend of mine has experienced this ghost in this room, she was lying down trying to sleep in the lower bunks in the room. Her boyfriend was downstairs with a few other ghost hunters at the time, when she heard something move in the room and then something stroke her arm. She said it was like being stroked by a soft blanket and she assumed that it was her boyfriend. It stopped after a second or so, and only then did she realise that there was no one else in the room. Suffice it to say that the pair of them did not sleep in that room that night, and swapped with a couple of eager ghost hunters hoping to get touched up in the Guard room.

Now hopefully we have time for a weird little experiment using the mirror in the Guard room, you need to be able to dim the lights in this room, or better still wait until it is dark, and then use a torch with the bulb covered in a piece of paper to give off a diffused glow and not a beam.

Sit comfortably in front of the mirror with the torch glowing into the mirror giving enough light reflecting back to see your face. I suggest only doing this experiment if there is someone there with you to keep you from doing anything stupid.

Scrying

This is a technique that trance mediums are known to employ to try and get a spirit to talk through them, or communicate with the dead in some form. I show people how to do this when I run Ghost Nights at the castle, but you must remember that I show people how to do all these experiments without necessarily believing in the experiment itself. Scrying on the other hand, is a great one to do because it does actually work. Whether it actually manages to communicate with the dead, or spirits is a different thing altogether, but it is a weird experience and worth trying at least once.

Now that you or your ghost hunting colleague is sat in front of the mirror you need to stare at your reflection, the idea is not to stare intently at yourself but to relax almost as though you were staring at one of the 3D magic eye pictures of dolphins. So stare through the mirror and do not feel as though you have to focus too well. So if you wear glasses it is not important to wear them, unless you are completely blind without them.

The idea is to allow whatever spirit is in the room to take over your face and try and communicate with your subconscious by allowing your eyes to see a different face staring back at you. This happens by reforming your perception of what you can see, and after a short period of staring at your reflection, you will notice that your features will start to disappear, for some it is one of their facial features starts to alter, for others it is that their entire face goes black and dissolves. This can be quite disconcerting the first time you try this, and you must persevere through this stage, relax more and allow this to happen, do not try to focus, as this will destroy what is happening.

Eventually you will see the features on your face change, and often a completely different face will appear, if you are lucky the mouth of this face will start to move as though trying to talk to you, so if you can then lip read what it is saying, so that your ghost hunting colleague can write it down. If you manage to relax enough then the entity may even talk through you audibly.

When we have done this experiment several faces are very common to see, firstly there is what people describe as someone that looks like Johnny Depp in the Pirates of the Caribbean films. They say they see a pirate style face with a goatee beard, don't get too excited though this is not the grabbing ghost, so before you hope to be grabbed by Johnny Depp whilst lying in bed, this figure only ever appears in the mirror never as a full apparition. Another figure is an old lady that looks like she has had a stroke. The right hand side of her face seems to have been affected in some muscle paralysis. The first time this 'face' came through we had a psychic artist by the name of Stephen Cox, (www.stephencoxart.com) giving a demonstration at the other end of the castle and he seemed to draw this face at exactly the same time as we were seeing it in the guard room.

The figure in the doorway has been seen by people doing this experiment, and also not only have peoples faces changed but the room itself takes on a completely different appearance in the mirror. I was scrying with a group on a Ghost Night and the gentlemen doing the scrying said that he could not see any difference, all he could see were the six people behind him reflected in the mirror. At which point I counted and there were only five of us.

One thing that happens regularly whilst I take groups scrying is that we often hear someone or something in the Hanging room, even though we know full well that there is nobody in there. We often position someone 'On Guard' looking into the hanging room, to make sure that there is no one walking around in there. The noises we hear tend to be the sound of furniture moving, people walking around, and also voices. People that have been in the room below the Hanging room (The Prison) have also said that they can hear people walking around and moving furniture, when we are doing the scrying experiment.

I do have one word of warning about this experiment which is that it can be highly addictive, I am not saying whether I believe in its ability to contact the dead, but I have seen it work, one guest was sat scrying, and she came flying off of her stool. I thankfully managed to catch her before she flew sideways and hit the floor, she claimed that something had grabbed her and tried to throw her to the floor. Like Ouija boards this practice ca be very addictive, so do not do it for too long otherwise the lines between reality and fantasy can get blurred very easily.

I would also suggest you do not try any of these experiments if you are in the slightest bit worried about them. The very fact that you are worried about them is enough for me to think you should not be doing them. I have never seen anyone come to any harm through parapsychology and ghost hunting. I will say that people can do themselves a great deal of psychological harm if they are not capable of knowing when to stop, and what is real, and what is not. We would like you to leave the castle thinking what an amazing time you had, and not in the back of a van with a straight jacket on.

*

Now I think it's time to head into the Hanging room, so walk through the doorway into the room next door, and a good idea is to find a stool and sit in either one of the window alcoves. Facing out towards the room, if there are two of you how about one of you sitting in one of the alcoves reading out loud all the stories, and the other sitting in the other. There is a reason for this that will hopefully become clear as we get through the stories of the Hanging Room.

More Footsteps

The most likely paranormal experience you will have in this castle is hearing and listening to footsteps walking beside you. The sceptical types all say well perhaps it was the sound of someone in another room, or it was someone walking by the castle outside in heavy boots, and you thought that it was in the room. There is a world of difference in the sound of someone walking outside, and someone walking within a foot or two of you.

When you hear these footsteps you can perfectly easily tell where they are coming from, and many witnesses can all point to the same place and say what they can hear.

The Neck Toucher Strikes Again

We had a neck touching ghostie in the Chaplains room, and the Chaplains room is only through the fire exit, please do not open these fire exits as they will then set off all the alarms. So could it be that this is the same neck touching ghostie. Unlikely is the reply as this one likes to touch you slightly too hard, the feeling of being held around the neck is not a pleasant one, yet you may experience it if you try sleeping in this room. The ghost here does tend to grab you by the shoulder more than strangle you, so perhaps I am wrong and in reality the strangling was a missed attempt at grabbing your shoulder.

Many people tell the same story of something grabbing them, they all say it feels like a hand just squeezing them on the shoulder. This spirit has been known to affect people in the Guard room as well.

The Pusher Part Two

I have experienced the pushing entity from the Guard Room, and hopefully if you did not get pushed whilst in that room you might in this one. People who have sat in the alcove on the left as you walk into the room say that they have felt something push them forward, as though they should not be sat there. Perhaps that is the favourite window seat of someone who was about to be hanged and you are obscuring their view.

Many people have reportedly been executed in this castle, and many of the rooms were holding cells for the condemned, in the hanging room you are closest to where these people were executed, as they were reportedly hanged from beams that jutted out from the front of the castle towers.

The Shadow With a Voice

I was in a ghost hunting vigil one evening and heard a strange noise off to my left. I was sat on one of the beds in the middle of the room facing the front of the castle. On my left between myself and the window alcove I heard a strange noise, at exactly the same time another ghost hunter thought they saw a shadowy figure in exactly the same place, about two foot to my left.

We were recording in the room using microphones and digital recorders, and when we played back the recordings we heard a strange voice saying something strange and incomprehensible.

Thankfully the recording has both our voices on and you can tell it is not us, but the voice sounds female and the only other person in the room was John a fellow ghost hunter from the Parasoc ghost hunting group in Cheltenham.

BOL's and Mist

The Balls of Light that travel around this room, are rather impressive, one of the BOL's is technically not a BOL, as it was a strange cylindrical green floating light. I am hoping that you are reading this whilst sat in the window alcove at the front of the castle. I was sat in the same alcove with a novice ghost hunter, she happened to be holding a night vision camera and was staring at the screen. The fact that she was staring at the screen meant that she was unable to see what I was looking at, this green floating shape floated along near the wall and eventually touched her shoulder. I was unable to speak, not for any paranormal reason but more because I was in shock, it lasted only a few seconds but was rather bizarre, and as soon as the green light touched my ghost hunting colleague she turned to me and said,

"What did you do that for?" I asked her what she was talking about, and she said that she felt me grab her on the shoulder. I showed her my hands in front of me to prove that there was no way it could possibly have been me. I then explained what I had seen, and I continued to explain to her as she left the room rather hurriedly.

Other BOL's have been seen in this room, and tend to be of the more traditional round variety, they are mostly seen above the beds closest to the doorway, and can be seen in both rooms. The bed on the Hanging Room side of the door however not only has small lights appearing, but also a strange mist, this mist has been seen in the Guard room but nowhere near as many times as it is seen in the hanging room.

The Tapping Window

One of my fellow ghost hunters told me of a great story in this room, He (Dave) was sat in here with two other ghost hunters, John and CJ from the paranormal research group called PARASOC. We often spend the night in the castle before we run a Ghost Night, taking baseline readings and setting up cameras and recording equipment. On this night we had a group in the hanging room, and a group at the other end of the castle, and there was no one else in the building.

The guys in this room were sat on various beds and boxes, and in the window alcoves. One of the group were sat on one of the boxes at the end of a bed, and a loud noise seemed to come from the box that he was sat on. This was shocking enough but nothing compared to what happened next. The window at the front of the castle suddenly had a tapping noise coming from it. It was the kind of noise as if someone was outside and knocking on the window.

If you take the time to look out of the window you will see there is nothing in front of the window the create this noise, no branches to knock the glass and you are stood a great distance from the floor outside, someone would have to have forty foot long arms to be able to knock on the glass.

All three of the ghost hunters said,

"What was that?" leading them all to think that none of them was responsible for either noise. They decided to all swap seats as even though they all trusted each other not to fake activity that would rule out any suggestions of foul play. Lo and behold the tapping was heard again at the same window this time with a different person sat in front of the window. When they all moved around again a knocking noise was heard from one of the boxes in the room.

This seemed to respond to their requests for something to happen, yet when they tried to get whatever was in the room to repeat its actions one more time, they were treated to a loud banging noise as though something had been dropped into the middle of the floor and even created vibrations through the floorboards.

Witnesses From Foreign Fields

It has taken me several years of investigating the castle to decide to write this book, one reason for the delay in writing is that we have not wanted people to know the stories. I have for several years run amateur, and professional ghost hunts in this castle, some open to the public with first timers coming along, and other nights when professional ghost hunters come along with thousands of pounds worth of equipment and try to record the phenomena. All this has been done with the help of Parasoc a Cheltenham based paranormal investigation group, and another group called Phantomfest, and my own group www.ghostnight.org who run the nights that are open to the public. We have succeeded in keeping most of the ghost stories from the internet and public knowledge, this way when guests turn up they do not know what to expect. Many ghost sightings can be easily influenced by what you are expecting rather than by what is actually there. So I find the most reliable stories are from people that come along and know nothing about ghosts or haunting associated with the building.

My favourite apparition story about the castle is one just like this. A Canadian gentlemen was staying at the castle as a normal paying guest, not a ghost hunter. He awoke in the night to see what he described as a woman in period costume walk across the room and kneel down, after a short time she disappeared. He told the castle staff about this first thing in the morning and apparently looked rather shaken when he did.

This guest apparently was not as scared as a Spanish student who stayed a month later. There were a group of students staying in these rooms and he awoke to see what he described as the same figure behaving in the same way. He did not know of the previous story as the only people who knew about that were the castle managers. They told me that the descriptions given were identical and they could not see how a Canadian man, and a Spanish student would have colluded to come up with a ghost story to tell two people who work in a castle on the Welsh border. If they had got together somehow, not only were they unusual joke players, but also fantastic actors as apparently the Spanish student was particularly disturbed by the whole event, and was in tears over the whole affair.

What a Mess

I am often called into houses to investigate haunting, and other phenomena, and for us ghost hunters we would all love to have a house with a resident ghost. We love ghosts so much that we forget how annoying they must be for other people. One such annoying spirit features in our next tale.

A previous manager told me that the hanging room has an annoying poltergeist, he was up there one day, and was making all the beds up for a group to come and stay. Youth Hostel policy nowadays is that they put the duvet and pillow covers in a plastic bag and you put them onto the duvets and pillows yourself, but back then this was all done for you, unfortunately budget restrictions mean its all self service now. So when he had finished doing all the beds he disabled the alarms and headed out of the hanging room and across a small bridge to the Chaplain's room. (If you are stood outside in the Gatehouse area look up towards the front of the castle and you will see this bridge linking the two towers.) He then made up all the beds in the Chaplain's room and headed back across the bridge back into the Hanging Room.

FOR ALL OF YOU READING THIS BOOK -
PLEASE DO NOT OPEN THE FIRE EXITS UNLESS THERE IS ACTUALLY A FIRE!

On arrival in the Hanging room he was rather shocked to find all of the duvets and pillows had been thrown off the beds and onto the floor, I am not sure if he put them all back onto the beds, or ran out and delegated that job to someone else later on that day.

So you don't have to open the fire exits this is what is on the other side of them

The Moving Beds

We have ghosts that move things around a lot in the castle, and they seem to favour the movement of furniture a great deal. One ghost has moved many items in here, and I have heard it do so on many occasions. I have recordings in this room when the doors have been locked, and there is no one in the castle, and when we play them back you can hear footsteps and the sound of dragging furniture.

The beds in this room have been known to move sometimes with people on them, I know of one ghost hunter whom I would trust implicitly that was sat on a bed as it moved. One of the castle managers told me of an incident where they had gone around the castle and tidied up, including the hanging room, and a few hours later they were walking around the castle showing a potential group of guests around. School, and youth groups often come here so this is not unusual to show people around when there is no one staying here. As they walked into the hanging room the manager realised that something was amiss. One of the beds had moved about a metre from where they had left it.

I must point out that no one had been in the castle, there were only two staff who had both been accounted for, and both say that they did not move the bed. These two were new staff to the building and did not know any of the stories about what goes on, it was only after they told me this tale that I then showed them my notes stating that this was a regular occurrence.

Heavy Breathing

Seeing a ghost can be quite a disturbing feeling, but I much prefer to see a ghost, than just hear them. If you can see where a ghost is and it is a scary one, you can avoid it, and walk around it if you need to escape. When you just hear a ghost you don't know where it is, or what it is going to do next. Well in this room there is a rather disturbing entity that likes to breathe heavily in your ear, it also has been know to Murmur and whisper to people. We have recorded voices in the room, often too faint to work out what is being said, and the heavy breathing is often very close right into one ear, some guests have even said they could feel it, as well as hear the noise.

Hahaha

Whilst we have been in the hanging room, we have heard laughter coming from the room below us. The Prison is directly below the hanging room and noise travels easily through the floorboards. We knew at the time that there was nobody in the Prison room. Not only have we heard laughter from the Prison, but people in the Prison have heard the same coming from above them, when there has been no one in the Hanging Room.

The most annoying thing about this haunting is that every time it occurs you have to run up and down the stairs to see if there is anyone there. Ghost hunting may be a good way of keeping me fit, by the looks of it.

The Moving Box

Whilst sat on one of the large wooden boxes that are often found at the end of the beds, people have reported the box moving, sometimes as much as several inches. Now in my experience we ghost hunters are often rather heavy, and for something to move a large wooden box a few inches with me sat on it would be quite an achievement.

The Shadow Moves

Whilst a group were scrying in the Guard room, a noise was heard coming from the Hanging room, so a couple went to the doorway to see if there was anybody in there, and saw a shadowy figure move across the room from the first window alcove towards the fire exit. They then tentatively looked around the doorway into the room, and saw nothing. No one in there, and no way that anything could have left the room without passing them or setting off the fire exit alarms.

The Footsteps Upstairs

One intriguing story is from the space above these rooms, often footsteps are heard walking around on the ceiling, and strange scraping noises have been heard going across the entire ceiling.

Above the Hanging room, possibly another haunted room, or somewhere with very noisy heavy

spiders clumping around in large boots.

A colleague of mine told me a tale of how he was lying in bed and heard something dragging across the ceiling and stopped directly above his head, (he was on the top of a bunk bed). When the dragging noise stopped he heard a scream, and assumed it came from someone that was having a nightmare in the next room. Soon after this people woke up, and the nightmare was quickly forgotten about, but he could not explain the dragging noise at all.

This story has been repeated to me a couple of times now by different witnesses, and one report we found goes back about fifty years of a similar incident. So if you are wondering what is above the guard room and the hanging room, we have an attic space, where there are not enough floor boards to be able to drag anything around.

The hanging room and its haunted moving beds

Flashers In the Hanging Room

This is a rather typical report that I have often been given by ghost hunters, this one was from a ghost night back in 2009 -

"I had the torch on the floor and left it there and it was flashing dimmer through to brighter, whilst it was on the floor, and no one touching. It was responding to us asking to let us know if there was anyone in the room, we requested the torch to respond by making it go brighter and dimmer and it did. We opened the torch and the batteries were red hot, this was done with three sets of batteries all different types, and they all overheated. The next night I was using the same torch and it was absolutely fine."

Pinch Me Please

Another common occurrence is the pincher, this ghost goes for the legs mostly, so perhaps it is a very short ghost pinching peoples legs, or maybe the ghost of a very large lobster. We shall never know, it is a question that can never be truthfully answered.....

Alright then I think we can take a guess that it is not the lobster at least.

Phantom Footsteps

The castle has hundreds of heavy footed phantoms walking around, and there are countless reports of ghost being heard walking up and down the staircase, we have experienced this on many occasions. One perfect example of this is when we had a group in the guard room and heard someone walk up the stairs and then the footsteps stopped outside the door, I walked over and opened the door thinking that some shy person was on the other side, not wanting to disturb our experiment, or vigil.

When I opened the door there was no one there, yet in the guard room there were about ten witnesses who all swore that they had heard someone walk up the stairs.

The stairs leading into the guard room from outside the prison

The Guard Room Blue Flasher

During a scrying event, there were about ten people in the room, a blue/white flash went across the room, all the people in there reported seeing something yet no one could agree on what the light flash did. After much discussion it seemed to travel across the room, and somehow settle on me and then go out. Obviously I didn't see the light land on me as I do not have eyes in my stomach, and as my mother says my eyes are often too big for my stomach, this is definitely true.

Chapter 5 - The West Tower
The Prison

Welcome to the Prison, we hope you enjoy your stay here, and do not feel too intimidated by the amount of condemned prisoners that have also shared this cosy little abode. May I suggest sitting in the window alcove that is the first on the left as you walk through the main door. As you sit here and look across the room you will see the fire exit, and yet again I warn you please don't open these doors. Also you will see the large fireplace to your left, and normally about eight beds in here.

If you look on the walls you will see graffiti carved into the walls, please do not add any of your own, this graffiti is actually part of the listed building, and of great historical importance. A school party staying here nearly had the castle closed down, and criminal prosecutions were made due to a child scratching something onto the wall.

It is thought that the pictures of windmills were carved by Dutch prisoners that were held here, and in the second window alcove you can see a curse that is carved onto the wall. In the first window alcove you can still see where the manacles were attached.

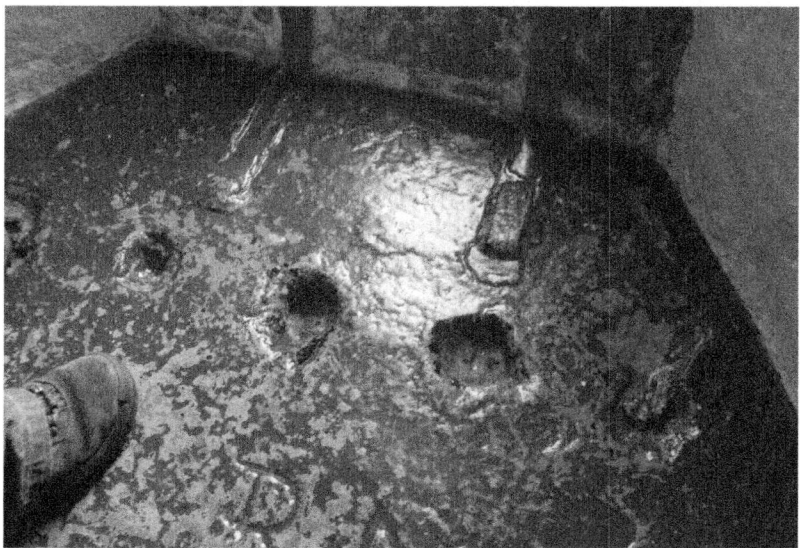

Where Prisoners were secured

Footsteps Again

As we have previously heard, there is a large amount of walking around and furniture dragging to be heard in the Hanging room, but the best place to actually hear all this is in the Prison.

One of the best examples of this I personally experienced, I was staying in the castle on my own, and had just locked up all the doors and windows. I still had the keys in my hand, so I knew that no one else could have got in whilst I was doing my walk around. I happened to be sleeping in the Prison due to the fact that the groups we were having in the next few nights were sleeping in the other rooms. So I settled down in front of my laptop with a good film to watch, a pizza in one hand, and a bottle of 'Diet Iron Bru' (I add that detail just in case you thought it may have been vodka, or scotch - I was totally sober). About ten minutes into my film I heard a noise I dismissed it at first thinking it was something on the soundtrack to the film, then it happened again slightly louder this time. I heard the distinct sound of about two or three footsteps directly above my head. I paused the DVD and listened thinking, or hoping that I was mistaken. There was nothing; my rational brain started to kick in and I thought I must have imagined it or it was a mouse, (albeit one with particularly heavy boots on!). As I reached forward to press play once more I heard the footsteps again this time three or four of them walking above my head, and then the sound of what I thought was a stool being dragged along. I would like to tell you at this point I jumped to my feet and ran out of the room up the stairs and into the hanging room to see.... Well nothing because I was too scared to do that.

No instead I did what anyone would have done if they were sat in here on their own I reached into my bag took out the headphones and plugged them into my computer putting the volume on full so that I couldn't hear it any more. Admittedly I should have gone upstairs just to check that we did not have any unwanted guests in the castle, but my nerves got the better of me, and lets face it if it was a burglar I don't think that a Youth Hostel has many things worth stealing, the family silver in reality is cutlery from the supermarket, the precious heirlooms are items left by forgetful guests, and the well stocked ancient library are books that previous guests couldn't be bothered to take home with them.

Now I am not the first person to hear these events, and I have been in the Prison with many a ghost hunting group, and heard this happen again and again. We have even recorded the footsteps in the empty room above knowing that there is no one up there. It is an amazing paranormal happening that occurs so regularly that if you are on a ghost hunt and have managed to be here on a night where the castle is rather empty and there is no one in the hanging room then try and request this room. If you are brave enough then send one person upstairs to sit n the guard room and check that no one is walking in there and making the noises. Good Luck!

Graffiti on the walls in the prison

The Moving Wardrobe

Whilst the castle is not booked throughout the quiet winter, this is your best time to try and come and do an investigation, but there are days when nobody is booked to stay and the castle is empty. On one such week five days had gone past without a single guest, and the castle staff did not even enter the castle as they were off on a training week somewhere about one hundred miles away. When the castle staff returned they walked into the Prison and noticed that one of the wardrobes had moved about a foot or so from its original position, now these are not heavy solid oak items of furniture I grant you, but they are heavy enough to be able to sit still in an empty room, in an empty locked castle. There was no obvious method of movement, as a slight breeze through the ill fitting windows would hardly be enough to move a feather let alone furniture.

The moving wardrobe, that has been moved sometimes as much as a few feet to reveal the carvings of windmills left by one the previous prisoners

Voices from the other side (of the fire exit)

During one ghost evening we had a group of people in the Prison, and when they left the room I asked them if they had experienced anything unusual as I always do. They told me that they had not, and I told them that there had been no one upstairs so if they had heard anything up there it would have been unexplainable. It was late on the ghost hunt and this group had experienced nothing so I think I was hoping more for their sake than mine that they had heard something.

They told me that they had not experienced anything all night, and the only voices that they heard were stood on the other side of the fire exit and must have been in the Constable's room. I thought they were saying that the people in that room must have been noisy and that they were complaining, so I decided to find out who was in the East Tower. It turned out that the East Tower was empty as most people were joining in with a table tipping experiment in the chapel and the King Johns Lounge. (Table Tipping is a form of séance using the movements of a table or chair to communicate with the spirits)

When I asked them again about the talking the group told me there must have been people in the Constable's room as they said it sounded like someone was leaning on the door and talking to someone else, at this point I took them outside into the Gate house, and shone my torch up to the bridges that come from the fire exits. They were rather shocked as they realised that there was no room on the other side of that door, and that nobody could have been stood there.

The Dark Shadow

This dark shadow is slightly different as he tends to not be too solid compared to the other shadowy figures in the building. We actually have two dark figures in this room but I am concerned with the one that is in the first alcove window. Hopefully you are sat here and may experience our scary friend. This one appears as a dark mist, and occasionally this mist takes on a human form, it is seen sitting, or standing near the window, normally as you walk into the room.

Grabbed by a Ghoulie

Being grabbed by a ghost is a strange and unnerving experience it has happened to me a couple of times, but most of the time they tend to prod or push. The ghost that frequents the Prison is much more of a grabber than a pusher.

As I have mentioned the stories I enjoy the most are the ones we are told by guests who have stayed not knowing that the building is actually haunted. These stories are not tainted with previous knowledge and are often grudgingly given as the guest thinks we will laugh at them, nothing is further from the truth as a father and son found out whilst staying here.

After staying in the castle, these two guests in the morning reported being grabbed. The father was grabbed by the hand by an unseen other hand, and the son claimed to have been grabbed on the arm. These are not the only incidents reported of this type, normally it is people being grabbed on the arm, but a large amount of reports state there are people that get grabbed by the ankle or on the lower part of their legs.

I did mention that I have been grabbed a few times by the ghosts, and this is one of the rooms where this has happened. I was stood with my back to the wall in the prison on the left hand side as you walk in. It suddenly felt like something cold was holding onto my hand, and then it started to move my arm. Some people would obviously claim it is a cold draughty castle and perhaps I felt a breeze on my hand, well to all those people I suggest you close your eyes and get someone to hold your hand, and also get someone to create a cold breeze on the other hand, I can guarantee that you will be able to tell the difference. This felt as though a small hand had hold of me and was moving my arm. I have also stood in this room, watching one of the ghost hunters from Parasoc standing rather bemused as something was tugging on his jacket, it was moving as though something or someone had hold of it and was pulling it. The ghost hunters present found it utterly fascinating and riveting, the ghost hunter in the coat however found it rather disturbing.

If you wish to try and experience this ghost it is likely to touch you on the arm, and the best place to be stood is next to the main door as you walk in, or near the window alcove. Position yourself somewhere along that route and hope that the ghost decides to come along and play. As I always mention in my books if something happens then please get in touch if not with me personally then tell the castle staff if something goes on. The castle keeps a ghost log of unusual events and they pass it on to me.

Ghostly Growls

We have talked a great deal about dark shadows, well be aware that there are obvious causes for such experiences, there are cars going passed outside that creates lights on the ceilings and walls, and strange shadows and reflections across windows and doors. So always try and check out a strange shadowy figure it may just be a jacket hanging up or a light coming through a window. One dark shadow you may not want to investigate however is the one to be found in the Prison. This one makes a noise, which is always impressive, as a shadow can not make a noise and therefore implies that something else is actually there.

Bruce from Phantomfest, was in the Prison the first time that any of us experienced this noisy spirit. He thought he saw a figure stood by the beds near the fire exit. He tells us that like most vigils in the Prison the lights were off, but you will notice that light can come in through the windows, so you could still see the features of the room. The figure that Bruce thought he had seen eventually disappeared, proving that it was not an actual person as was originally thought. When they turned the lights on they noticed that where they thought a person had been stood there was a radiator against the wall and a bed pushed up against that making it impossible for anyone to be stood there.

This figure has since been seen by others, and on several occasions a growling sound has been heard from exactly the same place. Sometimes the growling happens without a figure appearing. I have had tales from people that have been stood right next to the noise as it happens. Most people say it only happens once, however this is normally because they are running out of the room and unable to hear if it happens again. The brave few ghost hunters that have stayed have reported it happening a few times in a row.

Phantom Breezes

We mentioned that in the Oubliette there are some strange temperature fluctuations, well this room has some equally unusual occurrences. In the Oubliette the temperature raises and drops in weird and unusual ways, in the Prison however the temperature seems to walk around as though it is an intelligent entity.

The temperature will suddenly plummet and then go back up again but you can follow a cold breeze around the room, as if you are following a person around.

BOL's

Of course we have the now famous BOL's in this room, yet in this room they tend to be of a blue or white tone, the blue ones seeming to accumulate more around the door area.

Not only do we have these BOL's but we also have some amazing performing Orbs in here. What has to be some of the greatest Orb footage I have ever seen was taken in this room. I walked in on a rather amazed group who claimed to have seen some great Orb lights. I have to admit I was rather nonplussed by the whole affair assuming it was probably something rather normal, and in reality it would be some dust or insects flying around in front of the lens.

They rewound their tape and pressed play, I was suitably impressed as I saw a small light go across the screen, and it looked better than any of the stereotypical small white lights.

"Not bad, not bad at all."

"That's not it!" they told me to keep looking, as that was just the start of it, then for the next minute or so I watched an amazingly bright orb fly and quickly change direction all around the room, and then come flying towards the camera getting bigger as it approached the lens. I was then a lot more impressed and had to tell them that was some of the best BOL footage I had ever seen, and normally night vision cameras don't get anything that good. They then informed me that they could see it with their actual eyes, and not just on the camera. Just my luck always in the wrong place at the wrong time.

Possibly not the best day to try and get a shot of the valley from the top of the castle

Chapter 6 - The West Tower
The Porter's Lodge / The Old Kitchen

As you walk out of the Prison you will see a staircase in front of you, head down these stairs to the Old Kitchen, and Porter's Lodge. You should recognise the Old Kitchen due to what is known as a 'Dog Spit' on the wall. By this term we do not mean that there is a large green splodge of phlegm on the ancient walls. No instead you will see what looks like a large Hamster wheel hanging from the ceiling, this is the 'Dog Spit'

At the time of writing this book, we had a print of what this would have looked like when it was being used, this is in a frame next to the window looking out into the Guard house entrance Hopefully this picture is still there, if not then I shall explain. This castle has undergone many changes and uses throughout the years and you are now stood in what used to be the Old Kitchen. To make sure that the meat on the 'spit' over the fire does not burn it needs to be rotated so there is always a different part of the meat facing the flames. To rotate the meat a metal skewer went through something like a wild boar and the end of the skewer was attached to a chain that in turn was attached to this wheel. A dog would be placed into the wheel and as it ran it would turn the meat.

You will also notice if you turn back around that there is the remnants of a previous staircase in the corner of the room, curving up underneath the wooden staircase, so as you can see this room has changed shape many times over the years.

In the opposite corner to the bottom of the stairs you will see a door this is the door into the Porter's Lodge, if you head through here you will see another door that leads you into this Dormitory. This room is very similar to the oubliette room, except that the gap under the floors of this room is not a thirty foot drop from which you can't escape. So sit down and make sure you have a good view of the Fire exit in the corner, this door is alarmed so please do not open it. (unless you are on fire then maybe we will let you off)

The Porter's Lodge

This room does not have a huge amount of ghostly behaviour attached to it, so if you want a good nights sleep then this is probably the best one to go for. Having said all of that, it does mean you have to go through the Old Kitchen to get to your bedroom, and that has some of the most spectacular haunting phenomena throughout the whole castle, so lets hope if you are in here then you do not need to go to the toilet half way through the night.

The Ever Opening Door

So stay in the Port's Lodge if you want a decent nights sleep, but do not blame me if the few ghosts that do inhabit this room wake you up. One of my intrepid ghost hunting colleagues by the name of Paul was woken several times by the most prolific ghost in this room. If you notice the fire exit you will see it is bolted at the top, so that the door cannot accidentally swing open of its own accord. This is therefore the perfect room when we run ghost nights to store all the ghost hunting equipment in.

The Ghost Night groups therefore use this as a staff bedroom, hoping to get some sleep. Paul was asleep in this room hoping to get enough rest to be able to do another all night ghost hunt, and was getting rather annoyed as he was constantly awoken by people coming in and opening the fire exit. He thought it was annoying and kept closing the door. It was not until later that we all realised that no one was actually going into the room.

I have sat in the room and witnessed the main door open and close of its own accord, but the best examples of this is when you hear the door from the Old Kitchen into the Porters Lodge open, and then a second later the door into the Porter's Lodge opens as though someone has walked in. I have not only seen this but also seen it work the other way around. The inside door opens and then seconds later the door into the Old Kitchen opens, as though the ghost has just walked out again.

Figures have been seen in the porters lodge sometimes by the main door into the room, and other times by the fireplace

I Can't Get Out Of Bed

There is a phenomenon called Hagging, sometimes also known as incubus and succubus. An incubus or succubus is supposedly a demon that can pin you to the bed and have it's wicked way with you. Do not book this room hoping that this will happen, as by all accounts it is a terrifying experience.

Science however seems to offer an explanation for this, it is all to do with sleep paralysis. The body is still asleep yet the brain is half awake. The problem this causes is that because the brain is half asleep and half awake it is still dreaming and the feeling of sleep paralysis fools the brain into thinking it is being pinned down. This has happened to a rather terrified gentleman that was sleeping in the Porter's Lodge one night. He had no idea that the castle was haunted, so there were no preconceived ideas about what to expect, but when he reported this he was rather convinced it must have been a ghost.

The Figure Near The Fireplace

We have another figure that has been rarely sighted, but seen on at least three different occasions. There is no solid description of this entity, yet again it is a misty figure, or dark shadow in the shape of a human. This time it is seen stood near the fire place in the Porter's Lodge.

I guess it must be cold in the 'Afterlife' as the misty figures are often seen stood next to fireplaces in the castle. This does seem to cling to the theory that a ghost replicates its behaviour that it did whilst alive, as there were no storage heaters, or portable oil heaters in the castle, so I assume that the warmest places would have been standing next to the fireplaces.

We could be witnessing 'Stone Tape' theory where the ghosts are recordings of behaviour running over and over again, or even the start of a 'time slip'.

Time Slips, are where the witness not only sees a ghost, or event that has happened before, but the environment itself changes. The walls can suddenly have a different wallpaper on them, or doors can disappear . Often these time slips happen outdoors, battle scenes have been described, or groups of people walking past in medieval attire. When the witness goes back to the place an hour or so later the whole area looks different with trees in different places, and walls where there were none. Perhaps if our witnesses sat here long enough instead of running out, then the whole room may have changed, as they find themselves transported back hundreds of years.

The Rolling Coin

After a very long evening of ghost hunting, I was lying rather tired in my bed in the Porter's Lodge, I was not the only person in the room, as there were two other ghost hunters in there as well, Paul and Victoria. All of us were hoping to get a decent amount of sleep throughout the day so that we could stay up all night and do the whole ghost night all over again.

All three of us then heard a coin rolling along the floor, not in our room, but in the Prison above our heads. We had not heard anyone up there moving around so Paul decided to head upstairs and check out if there was anyone actually in there. When he got there a group were still awake and had been doing a ghost vigil. He naturally assumed one of them had dropped the coin, but was rather surprised when they told him that they had all heard and seen the coin rolling towards them. Not one of them was stood anywhere near where the coin had come from.

The Figure in the Doorway

I was at the castle performing in a concert of musical theatre songs out on the lawn, and I was there for a few days setting up tents and PA equipment. During this time I often had people that were staying at the castle coming up to me and asking me questions,

One couple were staying in the Porters lodge and had the room to themselves, they inevitably started to ask me questions about the ghosts. We do not like to tell people the ghost stories until after they have stayed and its their last day or morning in the castle. This way it is not auto suggestion and an overactive imagination. So I asked why did they want to know about the ghosts. The replied that they had felt something, like a strange presence in the room as though something was touching them almost. I told them a few of the tales, but told them that they were in one of the most un-haunted rooms. I did however tell them it would be a good idea to always have a torch with them, as some of the rooms can be dangerous to walk around in the dark, and it is advice we give to all ghost hunters.

These tourists then headed out and spent the day in Clearwell Caves(also Haunted) and the amazingly picturesque woodland that is puzzle wood (also haunted). They went into Coleford before heading back and thankfully bought a copy of my book 'Paranormal Forest of Dean'. That may seem like a shameless plug but in reality I mention it because half of that book is about the haunting that go on here. Most of the stories from that book do feature in this one as well, but the other half of the book tells of other haunted places to visit whilst staying here. Whilst in Coleford they also bought a torch each, which proved rather useful.

Later that night, the wife of the couple woke in the night and heard what she thought was her husband walking around and moving something near the main door, she looked over and saw his figure in the doorway. She reached under her pillow and took out the torch and shone it at what she assumed was her husband, and asked what It was that he was doing. As she did this the figure in the doorway vanished, and she noticed her husband in the bed next to hers.

Dragging

There are a few reports of guests staying in this room and hearing something being dragged across the floor, most described something that sounds like a heavy sacked being dragged along a wooden floor.

The Crying Baby

Many nights at the castle are filled with ghost hunting groups as this building has gained the reputation of being what is possibly the 'Most Haunted Building' in the whole of the UK. When we run ghost hunting nights, it is often on a Friday or Saturday, and several of us stay the night before to be able to spend the day setting everything up for the vast quantity of guests that will arrive in the evening.

This does however mean that we share the castle with several other guests and families that are not ghost hunters, so we do our best to not let on what it is that we do, so as not to scare them or their children. In the morning however when they leave and we are walking around with our Staff tops on they wonder what it is we are doing. I have often given an impromptu ghost tour to a group of families and tourists, and enjoyed watching their jaws drop as I tell them about the ghost that haunts the bedroom that they had just spent the night in.

I was taking a group around the castle that had spent the night in the Porter's Lodge, when we got to the King John's Lounge I told them a tale about a crying baby. Do not worry I will tell you the tale when we get there. One of the guests commented on the story and jokingly said he must have heard the ghost as he had heard a baby crying in the night, but that the noise came from the Prison. He turned to a man that was in the group that had stayed in the Prison and said,

"but I guess that must have been your baby, perhaps it was being troubled by the ghosts in the Prison."

"We don't have a baby, I thought it must have been from your room."

"We don't have a baby either."

The jokey atmosphere suddenly changed as both families realised that they may actually have experienced one of the castle ghosts.

You can still see the original shape of the windows
with the arrow slits poking out above and below the window frame

The Old Kitchen

When you leave the Porter's Lodge, make sure you go out of the door you came in, and not out of the Fire exit, that way if it is open when we walk past later and it's open, we will know it was a ghost that did it, and not you.

As you walk out through the door you will see a window alcove directly on your right, it is a good idea to get an chair and sit in this alcove whilst reading this next section.

As you can see we are not allowed naked flames in the castle, due to the ridiculously huge insurance policy this building has. So soak in the historic accuracy of the electric candles hanging from the ceiling.

Your Friendly Neighbourhood Poltergeist - Called Tom

We have a young poltergeist that seems to frequent this room. He has been nicknamed Tom for one major reason, every time we have psychics and mediums turn up they seem to normally come up with this name. Very often people who claim to have no psychic abilities whatsoever and consider themselves very sceptical also come up with this name if asked to guess at one.

So what does Tom do, well unfortunately in my presence very little. From the 'communications' we have had through mediums it seems this child does not like people that look like me, and tends to favour being around women. I have been fortunate to see a few things happen but not as much as the women ghost hunters have.

Tom tends to like throwing stones around. Now when a stone is thrown by a human it will follow a ballistic curve, the same as a cannon ball, or tennis ball or anything that is propelled and affected by gravitational forces. Poltergeists seem to defy gravity, instead of things flying in a curve they fall straight out of thin air or travel perpendicular to the floor, then fall at a ninety degree angle to their original flight path. The stones that fall in the room seem to appear in thin air and then fall directly downwards.

One of the best instances of this was during a ghost night, there were about seventy people staying at the castle, and they were split into various sized groups. Several groups throughout the evening experienced the falling stones all these groups wrote down what had happened to them and told no one. At the end of the evening we all regrouped and told our tales of what had happened to us all, and during this we were all rather shocked to see we had the same stories happening to all of us. After this most of the ghost hunters ran into this room, with a total of about forty people all crammed into the old kitchen. They then witnessed the same phenomena again.

Stone have been seen bouncing off the tables and sofas

During one ghost hunt a form of impromptu séance was taking place and one woman said out loud that the stone throwing was impressive, but if it could throw stones then she wanted one thrown at her. Before she finished the request a small stone bounced off of her shoulder,

We tell ghost hunting groups this story at Theodora night when we are telling them the more common tales that go on in the castle. One woman after hearing this story went and sat on one of the sofas in the Old Kitchen and said out loud that it was all rubbish.. It was at this point that a small stone landed on the sofa next to her.

"Fair enough" she said, got up and walked out.

Now how do we know it is definitely a small boy called Tom, well we cannot be sure of the name we just call him that due to the fact that all the ghost hunting groups call him this. How do we know it is a small boy however? That is a question we can answer, because he has been seen. One witness was a previous castle manager, the castle often has school groups staying over, and one such day the school were leaving in a coach and the castle manager walked past the window of the old kitchen and looked through seeing a small boy sat in the room. She ran out to the bus and told them they had forgotten one of their kids. After a quick headcount it was established that everyone was on the bus, the manager then ran back to the castle thinking that there was someone in the castle that should not be. Of course when the manager arrived there was no one to be found. Since then the figure has been occasionally seen by other staff and guests.

A Handy Apparition

There is a ghostly hand and arm that appears coming down the stairs holding onto the banister. It is often reported as being a feminine looking hand.

More People Than There Should Be

Quite often this room is full of ghost hunters will lots of strange equipment, sometimes they start doing weird Ouija boar type things, sometimes they have more equipment than the average electrical store. More often than not the room is very dark with lots of people sitting in silence, waiting for something to happen.

If you are in one of these groups I suggest you count how many of you went into the room when the lights were on properly. I have heard many stories from groups who end up with an extra person sat at the table, who gets completely ignored as they assume it is someone sitting in the dark looking for ghosts like themselves. It is not until someone questions how many people are in the room, or turns the light on, that the figure vanishes,

I Said Get Out Of My Chair

We have a great deal of pushy, prodding, and poking ghosts in the castle and the Old Kitchen is no exception. Hopefully you are sat on a chair in the window alcove and reading theses stories out loud to a group of terrified ghost hunters. Failing this you may be sat on your own in a dark room reading this by the aid of torch light and listening to the screeching of hawks, and the haunting calls of the owls. You may not be sat here for very much longer though, as one ghost likes to sit here, and may forcibly push you out of your chair. We have received several reports of this happening, and most people find it not too scary but a rather strange sensation.

Pinch Me

If the ghost does not kick you out of its favourite chair then it might actually try and get you to move by pinching you. Guests have reported what feels like a hand grabbing them around the waist, or pinching them softly. Some guests said it was almost like someone was trying to tickle them.

The Sofa Sitter

A friend of mine was a definite non believer in ghosts, she came and stayed in the castle one evening, she was sat in this room with a ghost hunting colleague of mine. For several hours she had been actively saying how we were all deluded and that there was no such thing as ghosts that could move anything or touch you in anyway.

As they were in the middle of this heated debate they heard noises coming from one of the sofa's opposite them. They were sat facing the side of the staircase, and there was a sofa directly in front of them. It sounded like someone was moving on it, and when they looked closely it looked like someone was sat there. In reference to the last statement I do not mean that there was an actual person sat there, but that they could see the impression of the buttocks of someone as if someone invisible was sat there. Each time they heard a noise, the impression seemed to move as though someone was shifting their weight in the chair. For the rest of the evening our friend made no disbelieving comments at all.

This was not a one off, there have been many reports of this over the years

Lets Open A Bank

Well our ghost's do seem to like money, as do we all I suppose. So far we have had tales of coins being rolled over the floor,. This time our friendly little poltergeist decides to drop money onto the floor. During one evening in particular he was feeling particularly wealthy.

Throughout the night several coins were dropped onto the floor as if they had fallen from nowhere. There was a five pence, a two pence, and a penny dropped in front of various ghost hunting groups throughout the night. Each group that saw this said that none of them had done it, and that there was no logical explanation to explain where these coins had come from.

Whistlers

Whilst sat in the Old Kitchen and also in the Prison, people have reported hearing whistling coming from various areas of the castle, which would not be possible as the rest of the castle has been empty at the time.

Chapter 7 - The West Tower
The Upstairs Corridors and Stairs

Once you have investigated the Old Kitchen and Porter's Lodge, we need to move back up the stair case to the landing outside the Prison, there is normally a table and chair in this area, but do not sit there instead you will see a window at the top of the stairs and sit in that alcove, so you have a clear view of the Prison door the stairs and the fireplace.

The Rattling Door

A fellow ghost hunter by the name of Paul was with me when we witnessed the door outside the prison moving of its own accord. There was no one in the Prison at the time to cause the doors movement. I did not actually see the door move, I heard it, but Paul who was stood in front of me did indeed see it. Other groups have reported this same phenomena since then

People have reported noises on the landing outside the Prison when there is no one there, it sounds like people talking or walking around, and then it suddenly stops.

The window seat where Paul was stood watching the Prison door move

The Noisy Stairs

I was in charge of a scrying experiment in the guard room, and whilst this was going on I had a group doing a ghost hunting vigil in the Prison, one in the Old Kitchen, and another group in the corridor outside the State Apartment. During the experiment we heard noises coming from outside the guard room door and down the stairs, it sounded like there must have been people stood outside the Prison.

After a while we realised that the noises that this group were making were interfering with our concentration and that I should go and tell them to keep the noise down.

The fireplace on the landing outside the Prison, note the small orbs near the brass fireplace hood. Some people claim these are spirits (personally I think its more likely to be dust in front of the camera lens)

As I walked down the stairs I saw another group looking up the stairs at me, they inquired as to whether I was making the noise, and I replied that I thought it was them. It transpired that this was the group from the Prison, and they had heard things outside the room. As we were discussing this the group from the State Apartments came in and said that they had heard things at the same time. I went down the stairs and asked the people in the Old Kitchen if any of them had been up the stairs, to which (no surprise) they said they had not moved, and no one had gone up or down the stairs.

All four groups had heard things moving, and the noises on the landing outside the Prison. All could testify that the noises were not made by them, and more importantly there is no way that anyone could have got past any of these people without being seen, (unless they jumped out of the window, and this is an experiment I do not suggest any of you trying).

The Falling Stones

There are many reports of the falling stones in the Old Kitchen, but there are also a few stories of a similar incident happening outside the Prison. Most of the time the sound of stones falling is heard, and more often it is just the noise and no stones are found. There are occasions when the stones are not only found, but also witnessed by many people as they fall from nowhere onto the floor.

Chapter 8 - The Great Hall
The State Apartments / Corridor Isobel's room

Many Many Footsteps

There are more footsteps to be heard in the Great Hall. This part of the building is now split into several rooms, with the State apartments, Isobel's room, a long corridor, and a small staff room that is used when staff members have to sleep over. This is one of the oldest parts of the castle, and has a couple of stories attached to it.

If you are lucky enough to be staying in the State apartments you may be in for an interesting night, recently this has been one of the most paranormally active rooms in the castle. You can often be sat in this room and hear footsteps walk across the room, and sometimes you hear the sound of curtains being drawn back even when they are already open.

The best bed, from a paranormal investigators point of view, is the one directly on your left as you walk through the door,. There have been may reports from people who have slept in this bed, and they all seem to say the same thing. They are kept awake by something pacing around the bed. A colleague of mine was sleeping in that bed and I was in the bed nearest the window, I had a great nights sleep where as he had not. I assumed to start with that this was due to my extremely loud snoring keeping him awake. He however informed me that my snoring was the least of his troubles. He looked rather shaken so I asked if he was alright,

"I am never staying here again", was the short and rather to the point reply. I later learned that the footsteps had kept him awake all night. He didn't tell me at the time, as he was rather shaken by the experience. Not that I would have heard a thing as he was using the universal protection against ghosts, that being a duvet pulled up around your shoulders so that only your eyes are poking out of it. Ghosts may be able to walk through walls but we all know that nothing can get through a duvet.

The footsteps in the room are not your only concern however the footsteps carry on in the corridor and here they are slightly more annoying, for the ghost also scratches on the door and walls, and sometimes bangs on the walls as well. Guest have been known to complain about the behaviour of other people staying in the castle complaining about the walls being knocked on and footsteps outside their room all night. The look on their faces is often very interesting and bemused when we tell them they were actually the only people in the castle.

The Woman and Girl In White

The source of the footsteps and knocking maybe that of a figure in white, she is often described as a young woman, or girl. She is more often seen at the chapel end of the corridor than the tower end.

The side view of the castle with the west tower at the front, the State apartment window on the left with the battlements above it.

This figure has been seen by castle staff as well as guests, and my favourite story about this ghost concerns a member of staff by the name of Neil. One night there was a large school group in the castle and Neil was staying in the overnight staff room, (the door next to Isobel's room). He decided to go to bed around 11pm, and as he walked into the corridor he saw a girl wearing what looked like a long night gown. He turned to the girl assuming that she was staying in the state apartments and told her that she should be in bed by now.

Before he managed to finish his sentence, the girl turned and walked through the wall, at this point he found that sleep is very hard to do when you have so much fear induced adrenalin pumping through your body.

She is possibly the source of the footsteps in the State apartments and possibly the same figure that is seen walking from the door area across to the windows. The problem with this hypothesis is that the figure is often a dark shadow walking across this room, yet the girl is often a white misty figure, or when she appears like a solid real person she is in white.

The Violins

A lot of the older stories in this book were given to us by previous cleaners and staff at the castle, one such member of staff was a wealth of information, and she told me that she would go into the state apartments to clean, and be met with violin music that then faded out. At the time there was a string quartet that used to rehearse in the castle so she would assume it was them, until she opened the door and there was no one there.

The first window you can see on the left is the Isobel's room the one furthest on the right is King John's Lounge.

Angry Arguments

One interesting reoccurring phenomena is that of an argument that happens. It is heard in the corridor near the Chapel end, though is also heard outside the toilets directly below here next to the refectory. We have occasionally managed to capture rather muffled versions of this argument on tape, but it is never clear enough to make out any words.

Lights and Mist

In the state apartment there are often BOLS seen giving off a blue or white colour.

The Woman on the Battlements

As part of my experiences ghost hunting in this castle I get to go along to many other groups nights, as this is one of the most popular ghost hunting venues in the country.

One group told me of a story that I did not think was out there in the public domain, and that is about a white female figure that is seen above the state apartments. Sometimes this figure is seen through the glass section of the roof.

The view from the Battlements above the State Apartments

The legend has it that the figure is a mistress of King John pining for his return, She was supposedly so distraught that she threw herself from the roof into the moat and drowned. it is reported that the ghost has been seen with another figure pushing her off the battlements, quite possibly getting rid of a minor royal problem.

Phantom Pillow Flinging

I normally only note down things that happen more than once but this incident was such a good one I thought I had better tell you about it and it does actually relate to some other phenomena, so we can get away with it.

One ghost hunting group were in the state apartments and were encouraging ghosts to appear and do something, they suddenly felt rather scared and decided to leave the room. Arriving into the corridor they realised they were being silly and why leave if you are scared, they were after all there to try and see a ghost. So they turned back around to open the door that they had just closed.

There was a problem as the door would not open. After a great deal of shoving they managed to open it a small amount and saw that a pillow had been taken from the top bunk of the nearest bed and forced under the door making it impossible to open.

Other people have told tales of their pillow being removed from under their head whilst they were lying on it, and a friend of mine complained of having a pillow thrown at him in the night, though we think this may have been due to his excessive snoring, and an angry tired ghost hunter.

The corridor where the young girl is seen, but more often heard

Don't Touch Me

Whilst ghost hunting several people have reported being touched by unseen hands whilst sat in the middle of the room. One ghost hunter said it felt as though someone had placed the palm of their hand on top of his head.

Chapter 9 - The Main Castle
King John's Lounge

The Crying Child

One story you can find quite easily on the internet is that of a crying child. Rather unsurprisingly this is also one of the stories that the mediums come up with again and again. They seem to miss out all the stories that happen the most and somehow always manage to come up with the ones that feature heavily on the internet.

One way of catching out the fake mediums is the crying baby, they always say that it is in this room, and yes it is in this room, but it happens in various other rooms as well. The reason it is linked predominantly to this one is due to a rather gruesome discovery. When renovating the ceiling above the fireplace a body of a child was found wrapped up and placed into the ceiling.

The most comfortable chairs in the world. I often find ghost hunters asleep in here

Since the discovery of the body the crying ghost has quietened down a great deal, and there is also one massive problem with this ghost. For those of you who live in the country or fairly rural areas, you will be used to hedgehogs and foxes. Many times the police are called out to find a child that has been abandoned in the woods, and they know full well it is likely to be the sound of a hedgehog or a fox, and they can sound remarkably similar to babies crying. I know for a fact we have some very fat and healthy hedgehogs wandering around the grounds, as well as our fair share of foxes in the forest.

The Floaters

Yes we have more BOLS here, floating lights seem to congregate around the main door area here, and tend to be a yellowy orange colour. People get very excited about these things when they think they have captured them on camera, most of the time what they have photographed is dust too close to the lens. You have to realise these Orbs or BOLS can be seen with the naked eye and not just on night vision cameras.

If you can see a glowing light and then you manage to photograph it I would love to see a copy of the photo as these are much more impressive than the multitude of photos of dust and insects that I get sent from people claiming that they are spirit manifestations.

Red Roger

One story you may find on the internet is that of a spirit called Red Roger, so called because apparently he has red hair. I was told this by a few very expensive commercial ghost hunting groups. The only problem I have is that no one has seen this entity and they claim that he manifests as a dark shadow or by appearing as lights. This leads me to the question, 'How do they know he has red hair?'

With all that said we do have a dark figure in this room, although it is not so much a figure as a darkness that spreads across the room and has been photographed at times.

The figure aspect of this apparition tends to be more near the fire exit, but it is rarely seen in a human type shape.

The view of King John's Lounge from outside the Fire Exit

Don't forget to take a good look at the fire place

Notice the notches on the pillar at the fireplace, one legend has it that these are notches carved into the masonry each time that someone was convicted and sentenced to be executed

Chapter 10 - The Main Castle
The Chapel

One of the castle staff who claims he only really took on the job after experiencing the ghosts first hand, gives us an excellent story about a regular haunting that he witnesses.

The chapel looking more like its recent usage as a classroom that a chapel

I do need to explain a few things about ghost hunting nights first, many groups turn up and do weird things like Ouija boards, séances, and strange vigils to try and communicate with spirits. Personally I do not believe any of these things actually work, and in reality you are only communicating with your subconscious. That is why the Ouija board was developed as a method of subconscious communication rather than to communicate with dead people. So keeping this in mind many staff have seen many séances using boards and other methods here, and heard many names supposedly being communicated with. So without further ado, and in the member of staff's own words here is an account of a chapel haunting,

"It all started in the chapel one day, and I am presuming that it is the people that came through on a Ouija board that came through in June 2010. One called Elizabeth aged 8 and the other 5 or 6 but cant remember her name. They came through and were

talking about the years they died. I ignored these stories and supposed facts as it was from a Ouija board so it could have been people pushing a glass around and fooling themselves.

So as usual I thought it could be real or it could be gibberish. But a month later I came here working permanently and we were doing a tour of the castle for a small group, and we did the tour in the evening not the morning. We were up in the guard room, telling them a few spooky stories about the guard and the hanging room, we were explaining about the things that we had seen and experienced. Then we heard footsteps running up the stairs, we all turned around expecting someone to walk in through the door, but the footsteps came into the room, without the door opening, we heard giggling and playing, and it sounded like they were running around me, and where I was standing. was wearing a T-shirt and it kept feeling like something hot brushing on my skin and we could all hear them giggling, and then after 30 secs it stopped.

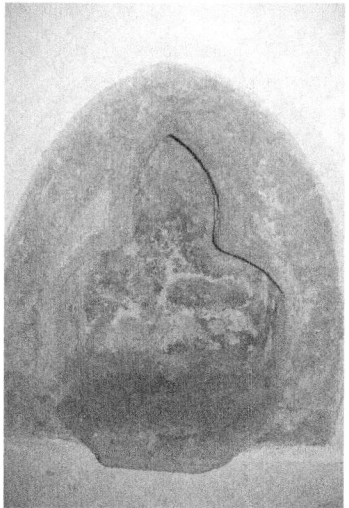

Evidence that the room was once a chapel - the remains of a piscina

The next time was about almost two weeks later, and I came in one morning at 7 and the hostel was closed and I had just come in to receive a delivery so there was not anyone else in the building at all. I was looking after the castle, and at 7:15 I heard a female voice so I thought it was the manager, as it was an English accent and female, I was not expecting her to be there at that time, and thought it was a bit early, when I stuck my head out of the kitchen door there was no one there. So I was confused at who had called my name, then I heard my name again, but this time it came from the top of the stairs, and I heard giggling. Then near the fire door at the top of the stairs I could hear the giggling from the chapel, as soon as I walked in it stopped again.

I realised it must be something paranormal happening, and then the third time was a *few weeks later again we were closed so I came around Sunday night. I was standing in the kitchen pulling things from the fridge and I heard the same voice calling my name and when I came out again into the corridor there was no one there, but the events repeated the same as the previous time by that point I wasn't scared. I said 'hello girls are you playing what are you up to today?'*

Another time Sue, (member of staff) has heard them calling out my name, even though I was not in the building."

Now the centre for many a corporate meeting, than a congregational meeting

Perhaps this member of staff gets some great results as he finds it perfectly normal to chat to the ghosts as though they are there. He even brought in some toys for the ghosts as an experiment to see if they moved them. This is not as weird as it sounds as it is a standard parapsychology experiment. I have seen evidence and heard witnesses say the toys have been moved when no one is near them or they are in locked rooms.

One medium who had no idea about the toys claimed to see a young girl telling her that this member of staff had her toys locked up in the staff bedroom. This was impressive for several reasons as the medium did not know about the toys, and also did not know that the toys were kept in a locked room. The medium gave descriptions, and said where they were, and even accurately drew the toys. This is one of the very few times I have seen any medium in the castle do something that cannot be explained with conventional methodology.

The Chapel Doors

Many groups have sat in the chapel doing whatever type of ghost communication they want to be involved in, whilst they do this they often report that something is trying to open the door to the chapel. They will sit there trying to get something to talk to them or move things to show it is there, at the height of these sessions the doors will open themselves or slam shut.

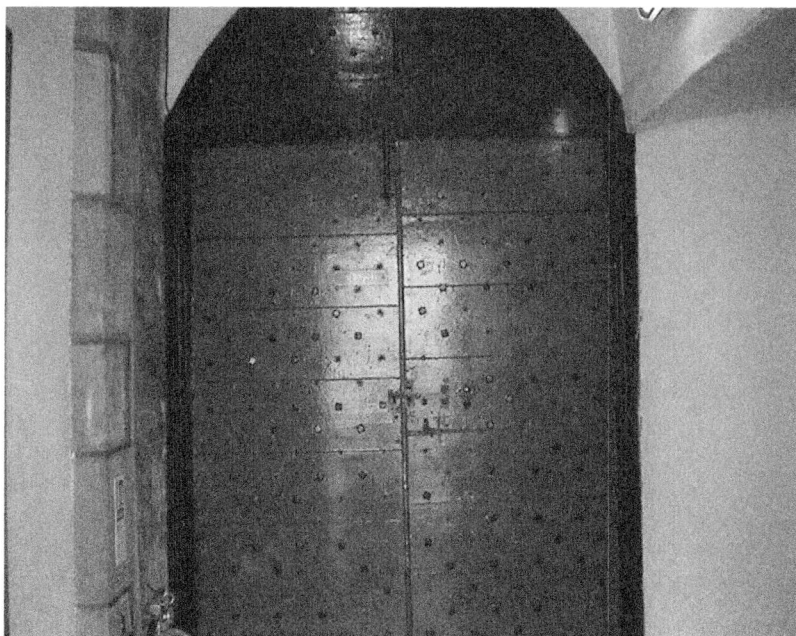
The Chapel Doors

The Noisy Ghosts

One rather annoying incident for the staff was when there was nobody in the castle and they were sat in the refectory. They heard a lot of noise coming from the chapel and went upstairs to investigate. When they walked in they saw that the tables and chairs had been thrown all over the place.

These incidents are great for parapsychologist, not so great for cleaners and staff who want to go home. It's very difficult to explain to an area manager why somewhere is rather messy even though you have claimed to have cleaned it up already.

Chapter 11 - The Main Castle Reception, The stairs, Corridors, and Toilets

Come on in - there is nothing that says 'COME ON IN, WE ARE FRIENDLY' more than weapons nailed to a wall

Name Calling

At least three previous managers have told me this story, it seems that the ghosts like to be on first name terms. Several people have reported being in the reception area and heard their names being called. The ghosts like to play with people as the members of staff often say they hear their name coming from the front end of the castle so they walk towards the old kitchen and then hear it coming from up the stairs. They then follow the voice along the upstairs corridor and back down the stairs and out to the reception again. The first time this happens they always think it is someone looking for them, then when it happens a few more times they start to ignore it. This gets reported from people in the main reception and also people who are in the kitchens and cleaning the toilets, and I know of at least ten different occasions of this.

Desperate for the Loo

This ghost is fantastic, because it haunts the men's and women's toilets on the ground floor near the refectory. Let's face it if a ghost is going to appear the best place for you to be is in the toilets when it gets too scary.

My brother is rather sceptical about the whole ghost hunting life that I lead, and he came along one night to a concert I was performing in at the castle. During the evening he went into one of the toilet cubicles, and whilst in there heard someone else walk in and then stop walking, he opened the cubicle door fully expecting to see someone in the toilets and yet there was no one there.

This is reported to me again and again, and I love this story because it is totally unexpected by the people that it happens to, all of them fully expect there to be someone in the toilets when they open the door. The very same thing actually happened to my brothers partner in the ladies toilets that evening as well. He left the castle that evening slightly less sceptical of the weirdness that is my life.

The Castle Pets

Obviously we cannot allow animals to run around the castle due to the nature of the building, but we can't stop the dead ones from running around. The castle has a ghost that is a dog, and a massive dog at that. It is often described as a large hunting dog, like an Irish Wolfhound type. The best version of this story that I know is from a ghost hunter that came to the castle and completely ignored the ghost thinking it was actually a dog.

Apparently the dog went down the corridor and he didn't even tell anyone. About an hour later another one of the ghost hunting party reported the same dog. The first ghost hunter acted rather relaxed and said that he had seen the animal, and what was wrong with that. He was rather shocked when told that there were no dogs in the castle.

The Most Haunted Staircase

This castle is full of ghosts that walk up and down the stairs, but the best staircase to experience anything is the one that leads from the ground floor near the main toilets up to the chapel and King john's lounge. I personally have heard people walk down this staircase and when I look towards the stairs there is no one there at all.

I have experienced this phantom sound on many occasions, and more importantly when there have been other people there to hear it as well. One of the managers told me how she had sat in the main reception and heard it happen about ten times in one day.

The footsteps are often heard coming down the stairs but not always, people sat in King John's Lounge, or the Chapel often tell of how they hear people walk up the stairs and stop but never hear them go back down again. These people rather confused go to look and see why there is someone stood at the top of the staircase, and of course there is no one stood there. I have heard this myself when I know the only other people in the castle were in the East Tower, and the gates were locked, so only people who knew the entrance door combination could have been there, as we had no guests staying.

Mind your head this castle is full of low ceilings, so perhaps we have the ghosts of people who lost their lives by knocking themselves senseless on the ceiling

One of my favourite stories about this staircase involves a fellow ghost hunter who was on crutches, she sat on the bottom step and heard someone coming down the stairs. She moved to let the person go past then realised there was no one there, yet she still heard the footsteps carry on and walk along the corridor. Even though she was on crutches she managed to move faster than most people do on two perfectly good working legs.

One member of staff told me how often she has been in the reception area and heard someone walk up these stairs so she went to look only to then hear someone walk up the stairs in the old kitchen so she went to check that out. She then got half way there and heard someone come down these stairs, so turned around and walked the other way again, as though the ghosts are having a game of human tennis.

Chapter 12 - The Main Castle
The Refectory, The Gatehouse, The Courtyard

The now walled up window above the fireplace in the refectory

Is It A Peeping Tom?

Well we can be pretty sure that this ghost is not Tom our poltergeist, as Tom is supposedly a young boy, this ghost looks older than that, but you will only get a fleeting glimpse of him, as he takes a glimpse of you. If you are sat in the refectory make sure you are facing the fire exit out into the corridor. If you are lucky you will see someone peer around the corner and then move back into the corridor towards the reception.

Several of my ghost hunting colleagues have seen him, and I have definitely heard him when I noticed one ghost hunter looking out into the corridor. I said what is it and then heard the figure move in the corridor. I ran to where he should have been and there was no one there. My ghost hunting friend was rather confused for a while but swears that he saw someone staring at him.

Several others of my friends report similar stories of a figure peeking round the corner then retiring back into the corridor. Each time when the corridor is examined there is nowhere for the figure to have gone to and if he did manage to somehow run up the stairs or down the corridor he does it completely silently.

The view out to the corridors and toilets where the figure peeks around the corner.

The best way of witnessing this is to sit at the second table and stare into the corridor, most of the times it has been witnessed, people have been sat there. I managed to jump over the table and get to the corridor in less than two seconds and yet the figure had vanished

The Rattling Doors

One ghost night we had a few people in the refectory and a few in the corridor next to the toilets, the doors were closed and latched. I was on the side of the doors in the corridor watching the doors moving. My friends were on the other side also watching it move.

We both watched as the latches on the doors moved and the doors shook yet no one was touching them

The door that not only rattled but the latches moved by themselves.

We had two teams of ghost hunters either side of the door witnessing the latches and doors moving of their own accord

Phantom Horses

Many people have reported hearing horses in the courtyard, often people are sat in the refectory and hear the horses walking past the windows. I myself have heard the horses walk through the courtyard heading out through the main gates. At this point I should explain there are no horses and it is just the sound of them.

Listen out for the phantom horses walking around the courtyard

The Floating Legs

One ghost is only half a person the lower half to be precise, as legs walking around on what would have been the first floor of the gatehouse are seen.

The view of the Gatehouse from the courtyard looking up at the ruined missing areas. This whole section would have been covered and rooms would have been here. The Gatehouse has several remaining gaps were portcullis would have come down to trap people in the killing zone. Each small doorway had its own portcullis. Anyone caught in this area would not have stood a chance.

The Banging on the Floor

One constantly re-occurring event is the noisy poltergeist that lives in the Chapel. The reason I have put this story in the refectory section however is that you only hear it when you are sat in the refectory.

When I run a ghost night, there are several of us who make sure the evening runs smoothly and at about 2am we all congregate in the refectory. Whilst I am sat in the refectory normally with a friend of mine called Paul taking notes we go over the evenings events. Then we tell everyone the stories in each room and see if it collates at all.

Whilst we are telling the stories the other members of the team walk around the castle to make sure there are no people hiding in rooms, or have been left behind in the kitchen or just stragglers taking ages to come back. This is all done to make sure that we know where everyone is at this given point.

Many times when we start telling people about the castle ghosts, one of them likes to make his presence known by banging around in the chapel, it evens makes strange moaning noises sometimes. Every time we send someone upstairs to check that there is nothing or no one up there the noises stop, then when that person comes back down again the noises start up again.

The Banging Doors

I was stood one evening telling people about the strange incident with the doors moving in the refectory. One person that was party to this conversation adamantly refused to believe me. Claiming that I was talking rubbish and that there was no such thing as ghost. It did not matter how much we insisted that we do not make up ghost stories this person was determined to remain on the non believers side of the fence. His protestations grew more and more until all of a sudden the doors to the castle flew open at great speed crashing into the walls.

The rather large heavy gates in the gatehouse. These doors flew open at great speed. Try moving them for yourself and you will see that it is not easy to open them quickly. Myself and a fellow Ghost hunter by the name of Paul spent a great deal of time and definitely effort trying to replicate the speed at which these doors opened. We failed miserably, and ended up with bruised shoulders from running into the doors trying to force them open at speed.

Knock Knock - Who's There?

One rather irritating ghost knocks on the castle gate, and when you open the gate it has disappeared. It does not matter how quickly you get to the gate there is no one there. I have been stood next to the gate, heard the knocking and within two seconds the gate was wide open, and there was nobody on the other side. Though I think I prefer that version than the times that people have opened the gate let someone in and then that person disappears, this has happened on at least three different occasions that I know of.

Try moving these doors. No breeze can make them swing open at such speed

Chapter 13 - The Castle Grounds
The Gardens, The Car Park, The George in the Moat, The Church Graveyard.

The Knight in Shining Armour

This ghost is everything a ghost should be, a real stereotype. Near the fireplace in the wall a figure has been seen, though not for some time. It is reportedly a knight in full armour as though heading out to battle. This story is one that you will find on the internet and is often repeated by mediums yet in all my years here I have not seen, or heard any reports of anyone seeing it.

What is seen however are two figures to the right of the fireplace, and I have seen these myself late at night. Unfortunately when we see someone in the grounds we do have to go and check out that it is a ghost, in case it is actually someone trying to break in.

A very rare view of the castle gardens taken from the battlements after a heavy snow storm

The Skulking Figure

During one ghost evening a few ghost hunters saw a figure between the fire exit of King John's lounge and the bike shed. The people who saw it ran away rather scared, so we quickly ran out to find the figure, it had gone in the ten seconds it took us to get there. We swept across the grounds and there was no one to be seen. Whilst we were looking around the moat to check there was no one climbing over the walls, these original witnesses returned. During this time they claim that they heard footsteps or something walking around them. The ground was very wet, and it sounded just like squelching footsteps, yet no one but this group were out there.

Where the knight in armour is normally seen, don't get too excited these stocks are reproductions not originals.

The fireplace is all that remains of the old courthouse that once stood here.

In the castle gardens looking towards the chapel.

The large stone to the left of the lower sheds is part of all that is left of the original Norman keep. Most of the keep has been destroyed and the stones that made it can be found in a lot of the older buildings, and gardens throughout the village.

There has been an archaeological dig of the keep and the cellars remain underneath the raised area of the gardens. All that can be seen of the remains are three large collections of stones and rocks often found with children climbing all over them on a sunny day

Ghost hunting can be a very chilly experience

The George - Situated in the moat of the castle

The Ghost That is George

This pub is haunted and if you are staying at the castle then it is an entire 30 seconds from the main gate. The castle in my opinion does excellent and cheap meals, but should you wish to broaden your choice of food then you could do worse than heading to the George for the food is phenomenal. Whilst there ask them if they have experienced any ghostiness recently, they will hopefully tell you about their resident spook.

This building not only has a ghost but they have his coffin lid set into the wall. One ghost hunter felt a phantom push her as she went to the toilets, a previous landlord told me about things moving, and figures being seen. This landlord told me that the pub was built over an old footpath and perhaps a lot of the ghosts are just phantom walkers exercising their right to ramble. The most common ghost he told me was a monk like figure that they have christened George, and that he had got so angry with it once that he opened the door and started shouting at it to leave him alone so that he could get some sleep.

The George - Located in the castles moat, it does excellent food, and when you get there, ask to see the coffin lid in the wall

The Graveyard

The best time to walk around the graveyard is in the day, but don't forget for some people this is a very sacred place, don't go wandering around covered in flashing lights, and carrying bits of the latest ghost hunting equipment

Normally I would tell people that you have nothing to be scared of in graveyards. For some reason people are very scared of graveyards and think they must be very haunted. If you look at most hauntings they are linked to places where murders have happened, or where people have died or lived. It is rare to find a ghost in a graveyard as no one died, or lived there.

There is however a tradition in some forms of Christianity that state that the first person to be buried in a churchyard will stay on as a ghost to protect the graves of those buried later. This is probably a story created to stop people coming along and digging up the bodies as grave robbers. A lot of religious superstition is often created to protect the church in someway, the pyramids had similar unfounded curses attached to them to stop thieves, for where ever there Is money there are thieves.

Now having said all this there is supposed to be a strange figure that skulks around the graveyard, peeking out from behind grave stones, and when you get closer you realise there is no one there, or anywhere for the person to have run off to. One member of staff from the castle has told me that they have seen the figure a few times, and that she does not like walking through the graveyard

Frozen Graveyard – Enter at Your Own Risk!

Only because it's very slippery on the ice

Other Village Ghosts

Recently I was told a story about the Mariana gallery just round the corner from the castle. One person was in the gallery and heard someone walking around in the cottage area of the building. They naturally assumed it was someone in there, and started talking to them as they thought it was a colleague of theirs. When they walked into the area they thought that this person was in, they realised there was no one there, and more importantly nowhere for this person to have disappeared to.

Another story I have been told of recently was a few fields from here, and dates back a few decades and I only include it because it lends some credence to some stories I have heard around the Clearwell area as well as St.Briavel's. Our witness told a story of how he had seen several people being lead across the fields in chains, from the descriptions he gave it sounds as though he witnessed a group of Romans escorting slaves towards the mining areas near Clearwell.

St.Briavel's Church in Winter

Chapter 14
What To Do If You See A Ghost?

Well first of all there is definitely no need to panic. This is obviously easier said (or written) than done. When faced with a glowing phantom that can walk through walls the instant reaction is to scream or run away. The ideal reaction would be to pull out a camera and take a photo, The best reaction would be to get a photo, and start taking notes whilst trying to communicate with the spectral form.

I am fully aware that none of this is likely to happen, I have been doing this for a long time, and yet I still do not behave in this manner. I may not always run screaming from the building but I certainly do get scared sometimes, and sometimes I forget to take a camera, or make notes.

What you can do if you are staying at the castle is to report it to the castle staff and they will jot it down in their ghost diary. If you see a ghost and you are not at the castle I am always interested in hearing about it so email me at

ghostnight@hotmail.co.uk

Even though I do investigate cases all over the country I might not be able to get to investigate your ghost in person. I may however be able to help and make suggestions about what you should do. So happy ghost hunting, and I look forward to your tales to be included in 'St.Briavel's The Most Haunted Building in the World - PART TWO

See You Soon

Chapter 15
Conclusion, Epilogue, and Rest In Peace

I am hoping that you have read this book and felt a slight chill or even the sense sheer terror, what I hope is that I have NOT altered your view and you now believe in ghosts.

Even though I believe in ghosts as I have seen many, and I have spent many years here in this unbelievable building witnessing time and time again phenomena that cannot be explained. What I hope is that the more sceptical amongst you may be slightly more open to the possibility of ghosts. Those of you who believe that ghosts are spirits of the dead coming back to life in some form, I hope you walk away thinking that ghosts are not just that, they may be many other yet to be explained things. A ghost is not proof of life after death, and the more ghosts I witness, the more I think there is no life after death, and that ghosts will be explained by science eventually.

So in the spirit of science keep an open mind, though not so open that your brain falls out. If nothing else I hope you enjoyed the book, and if you stayed at the castle I hope it is a good souvenir of your stay at what is possibly the -

WORLDS MOST HAUNTED BUILDING!

This may be the moat but its not frozen ice so no skating today I'm afraid

Chapter 16
More History

Over the years many of the bricks from the castle were stolen to be used to build the houses of the village. This lead to many of the walls having jagged unfinished edges. Most the rear wall of the castle seems to have been stolen.

As promised I thought I would include a section here at the back going into a bit more of the history of this magnificent building. It seems as though there has been a fort of some description on this site for nearly a thousand years, but let us limit ourselves to the structures that are made of stone, and can thus be truly called some form of castle.

It seems as though the instigator of this building was Milo Fitz-Walter, for in the year 1131 Milo claimed an allowance for certain expenses for the services of one knight, sergeant, porter, and a watch for the ,"Castellum de Sco, Briavel". It is likely that he had the stone keep built and the surrounding stone walls.

The castle is well known as King John's hunting lodge but he was not the only royal to grace the building with his presence. King Henry II was in the forest in 1158 and probably at St.Briavel's in 1164 as historic records indicate.

King John seems to be the most famous resident however and he has stayed here a minimum of six times. Records indicate that on the 24th February in 1205 he ordered two tuns of wine for St.Briavel's. on 13th November 1207 he ordered the Constable to buy more wine. On November 14th he was in Gloucester and at St.Briavel's the following two nights. On the 29th of March in 1209 he granted the town a market to be held weekly on Saturdays. He was also at the castle on Nov 10th, and 11th in 1212, and then again on November 28th to 30th in 1213. There is an old rhyming couplet which celebrates John's love of St.Briavel's

"St.Briavel's water and Whyral's wheat. Are the best bread and water King John will ever eat."

Henry II also seemed to frequent the castle at least twice, once in 1226,and once in 1228. It was however a very important building as he used it to manufacture arms. It was the leading arrow head factory, and in 1223 Henry used 6000 of them.

What is left of the castle, except for the gatehouse, was mostly built by Henry de Bohun between 1180 and 1190. The Norman keep, which was magnificent by all accounts standing at over one hundred feet tall and with walls that were eight foot thick, collapsed due to neglect in 1752, and by 1754 was completely destroyed.

The castle has had many uses throughout history not only was it an arms factory and a hunting lodge it has also been a court house, a prison and a place of execution. During the reign of Charles II the West Tower roof was altered and had rafters installed on the North West side projecting out of the building and probably supported a platform, or was just used for hangings.

The stone staircase was also removed from the towers at this point, as large alterations were made to the castle. You only have to look around you when in the castle to see that at no point has the castle managed to keep in one style. Nowadays buildings are kept as best as possible in their original design, but it is impossible to find an 'original' style within the surviving walls of the castle.

Charles' father Charles I still has a slight influence in the castle as it was during this period that the kitchens were built and the 'Dog Spit' in the Old Kitchen is an original dating from that period.

Connected to the Miners court (which was based at the castle) there was a Prison, which was visited by the famous prison reformer John Howard. And in his writings we learn of his visits to St.Briavel;s.

"St.Briavel's goal for Debtors. No Alterations (since his previous visit) The keeper sells beer, and there is company as at a common ale house. Here were lately released one who was confined near a year; debt on 3s., costs £4 11s. 4d.; another near two years, debt 40/-, costs £7 15s 0d.; another debt £1 19s., costs £4 4s. 6d." all of which puts my credit card bills into scary perspective. Another entry for January 31st in 1778 states a very brief description. "No prisoners"

There is still a great deal of graffiti left carved into the walls of the Prison by the prisoners. Including one more famous piece, craving revenge.

ROBING BELCHER
THE DAY WILL COME
THAT THOU SHALT
ANSWER FOR IT FOR
THOU HAST SWORN
AGAINST ME 1671

It was in 1758 that the castle was nearly lost completely as it had fallen into such disrepair that Elizabeth, countess of Berkeley wrote that there was not much left standing only, "a few rooms for holding courts for the Hundreds of St.Briavels, and business related to the forest, a prison, and for a keeper to reside in,". She goes on to say that it is, "in very ruinous condition". This was an attempt to instigate repairs, for she states that, "the courts cannot be held, nor can any persons be confined in the prison without endangering their lives."

In 1777 an estimate was made for repairing part of the East Tower which had fallen down, the tower had fallen and taken out a large section of the adjoining buildings. This had destroyed part of the kitchens and also ended up filling the dungeon with debris.

For over forty years going back before 1872 the building was a school. The Jury room had ended up as a carpenters workshop and a lot of the building had no roof, and the court room had ended up without a floor. So a great deal of work was then done to bring it into a habitable state once more. It was also used as a private residence for a while before English heritage gave the castle over to the Youth Hostel Association.

See You All In Part Two

Me in a publicity shot looking a lot scarier than any of the ghosts at the castle.

I hope you enjoyed the book, and whether you have bought it as a souvenir for the photo's, or you are staying at the castle and wanted to terrify your children, I hope you experience something paranormal.

You can always join us on one of our ghost hunting nights and see if can be a spook spotter.

If you get any more ghost stories to be included in our files please tell the staff at the castle, and they will add it to the collection. You may feature in the next version of this epic tome. If you want to send me the stories anonymously then email them to ghostnight@hotmail.co.uk

Other books by this author

Paranormal Cheltenham - Amberley Books
Paranormal Forest of Dean - Amberley Books
Paranormal Oxford - Amberley Books

The castle wall hiding behind the gardens as looked after by the Moat society

Don't get too excited we did not manage to capture the knight in armour on film. This was a photo taken on the castle open day of a battle re-enactor.

More scary Medieval re-enactors

The view up the chimney from inside the fireplace in the grounds

See you in Volume 2

Happy Haunting

First published 2010
Copyright 2010 TozMusic press

The rights or Ross Andrews to be identified as the Author
Of this work has been asserted in accordance with the
Copyright, Designs, and Patents Act of1988.

All rights reserved. No part of this book may be reprinted,
or reproduced, or utilised in any form or by any electronic,
mechanical, or other means, now known or hereafter invented,
Storage or retrieval system, without the permission in writing from the Publishers